LISTENING FOR GOD

Also by Teresa Tomeo
from Sophia Institute Press:

Conquering Coronavirus
How Faith Can Put Your Fears to Rest

TERESA TOMEO

LISTENING
FOR
GOD

DISCOVERING
the INCREDIBLE WAYS
GOD SPEAKS *to* US

SOPHIA INSTITUTE PRESS
Manchester, New Hampshire

Sophia Institute Press
Box 5284, Manchester, NH 03108
1-800-888-9344

www.SophiaInstitute.com

Sophia Institute Press® is a registered trademark of Sophia Institute.

Paperback ISBN 978-1-64413-302-6
eBook ISBN 978-1-64413-303-3
Library of Congress Control Number: 2020943279

2nd printing

CONTENTS

DEDICATION AND
SPECIAL THANKS

I want to dedicate this book to all its amazing contributors, whom I can call not only my friends but also my co-evangelizers in the vineyard. I encourage you to take the time to visit their blogs and websites, connect with them, and support their ministries. I want to give a special shoutout to Gail Coniglio—my literary agent, publicist, and right hand—who helped me compile all the stories, and to my wonderful team at Teresa Tomeo Communications—Gail, Marcy, Palma, Patti, Jeff, and Vanessa—for your support and for helping me in my ongoing evangelization efforts. Thanks also to the fabulous team at Sophia Institute Press for making this book project a reality.

LISTENING FOR GOD

INTRODUCTION

Call to me and I will answer you, and will tell you
great and hidden things which you have not known.

— JEREMIAH 33:3

Have you heard from God lately? I'm not a betting woman, but if I were, I would bet hands down that something has happened in your life that gave you the chills, made you do a double take, or caused you to admit that the incident was at least a coincidence or even perhaps what I like to call a "Godcidence." Maybe you were driving to work this morning thinking about a loved one who has died, and suddenly, you heard his favorite song on the radio. That was a hug from heaven in response to your heart's desire to reconnect with that friend or relative. You might have been at Mass recently and sat there feeling somewhat numb: really struggling with fear related to an illness, financial troubles, or a wayward child. Maybe you're still struggling, as many of us are, from the fallout of a very long and difficult period that included a pandemic, followed by economic uncertainty; an illness that came out of nowhere, only to be followed by yet more uncertainty caused by a level of civil unrest not seen in decades. It all seems too much to handle. And then you hear the readings, and they are spot-on, matching just what you were feeling. Yes indeed, that's God speaking. He loves each one of us so deeply that He will stop at nothing in His efforts to reach us using such a variety of means: people, nature, Scripture, music, and yes, even pain and suffering, to let us know that He is with us always, "until the end of the age" (Matt. 28:20, NABRE).

I wrote this book for two main reasons: first, because I have been there, done that, and bought one too many T-shirts to mention when it comes either to ignoring God completely because I had better plans and ideas, or to conveniently keeping the spiritual headphones on so tightly and the music playing so loudly that I would not have been able to hear God even if He were standing right in front of me shouting through a bullhorn. I was neither ready nor willing to hear His plan for my life. I understand this struggle from a personal and a professional perspective, since my ministry as a Catholic talk-show host, motivational speaker, and conference leader takes me all over the country and the world and introduces me to all sorts of people. It is very evident that so many people—even those with a deep faith—have strong doubts, are losing hope, and might even think they've been abandoned by God. They are frequently overcome by the ugliness of the world, especially the myriad challenges we have faced recently, including the attacks on the Church from within and without. They have a tough time believing the situation will get any better any time soon. This goes especially for millennials, according to a recent public health report:

> Drug, alcohol and suicide deaths have risen in nearly every age group over the last decade, but the increase has been especially pronounced for younger Americans. Between 2007 and 2017, drug-related deaths increased by 108% among adults ages 18 to 34, while alcohol-related deaths increased by 69% and suicides increased by 35%, according to the report [released by public-health groups Trust for America's Health and Well Being Trust], which drew on Centers for Disease Control and Prevention data.[1]

---

[1]   Jamie Ducharme, "More Millennials Are Dying 'Deaths of Despair' as Overdose and Suicide Rates Climb," *Time*, June 13, 2019, https://time.com/5606411/millennials-deaths-of-despair/.

Their ears are ringing so loudly from the impact of this despair that they can't hear God.

If millennials are not in a state of despair, they exist in what noted Catholic teacher and media evangelist Bishop Robert Barron calls the culture of "meh" or "whatever":

> Our society today is like a big lazy lake, all of us floating individually, tolerating each other, not getting in each other's way, but without energy, without purpose.[2]

But what if we were more tuned in to God's voice and what He is trying to say to us right now? What if we were more aware of His presence in our lives despite our circumstances? Wouldn't that make a major difference in how we lived? And in turn, wouldn't that have a positive effect that would reverberate well beyond our doorsteps?

That brings us to the second reason I wrote this book: from the stories of Godcidences shared by my friends and colleagues on the following pages, as well as my own personal encounters with His strong but still voice, it's my hope that you will be encouraged, uplifted, and affirmed by realizing that God keeps His word. These Godcidences, wherever, whenever, or however they occur, are signs of His reaching out to us.

So how do you know that it is really God talking? Great question. Indulge me for a moment: speaking from all the many fumbles and stumbles I made in my journey with God, I suggest that perhaps the more pertinent question is whether we are ready and willing to listen. The fact that you picked up this book is an incredibly good start. Now, let's think about what else we can do to welcome and appreciate God's voice.

---

[2] Catholic News Agency, "Bishop Robert Barron's six tips for evangelizing the 'nones,'" *Catholic World Report*, July 4, 2017, https://www.catholicworldreport.com/2017/07/04/bishop-robert -barrons-six-tips-for-evangelizing-the-nones/.

One major barrier could be our own self-esteem or lack thereof. We might think our past sins have kept us from hearing from God. We're not good or holy enough for Him to reach out. Well, quite frankly, if that were the case, none of the apostles would have made the cut. St. Matthew was a despised tax collector. St. Peter was a rough-and-tumble fisherman who would go on to deny the Lord not once, not twice, but three times. Oh, and let's not forget the fact that all the apostles, except St. John, would run, hide, and totally abandon Jesus when He needed them most, during His horrific death on the Cross.

If you're not quite convinced of your worthiness to hear from God, I encourage you to look at some of our other saints. Too many to mention lived less-than-stellar lives of virtue, and that's putting it mildly. For example, among other things, the great St. Augustine had a child out of wedlock while living with the child's mother, whom he never married. Augustine's time on earth spanned the third and fourth centuries after Christ—imagine the scandal he must've caused back then! In addition to his wayward lifestyle, he wandered spiritually for years, following all sorts of teachers and philosophers in just about every other religion before having his own profound Godcidence. To make a long story short, St. Augustine thought he knew better. Eventually, the brilliant orator and thinker humbled himself and allowed Christ to capture his heart completely. Augustine became a bishop and prolific Catholic writer, receiving the esteemed titles of Doctor and Father of the Church—titles given to those recognized for the significance of their contributions to the Faith.

Mother Teresa says in order to hear God, we need to have a "clean" heart. She does not say we have to be holier-than-thou, so to speak.

The beginning of prayer is silence. If we really want to pray, we must first learn to listen, for in the silence of the heart God speaks. And to be able to see that silence, to be able to hear God we need a clean heart; for a clean heart can see God, can hear God, can listen to God; and then only from the fullness of our heart can we speak to God. But we cannot speak unless we have listened, unless we have made that connection with God in the silence of our heart.[3]

A "clean" heart means a heart that is humble and open; a heart like Augustine's, willing to recognize who God is and who we are not. Or a heart like King David's. You do not have to be a Bible scholar or even all that knowledgeable in Scripture to remember David's dramatic as well as traumatic story. Most of us are at least somewhat familiar with his fall from grace and his eventual repentance: a turnaround that would cause Samuel and St. Paul to remind us that David was a man after God's own heart (see 1 Sam. 13:14; Acts 13:22). At times, David was not exactly in line for the Man of the Year award. After all, he made some pretty rotten choices, such as his move to send Uriah, his mistress Bathsheba's husband and his closest confidant, to the front lines of battle in order to have him killed. Yet David eventually came around, begging God to help him change his heart. In the Psalms, he prayed: "Hide your face from my sins, / and blot out all my iniquities. / Create in me a clean heart, O God, / and put a new and right spirit within me" (51:9-10).

In his weekly General Audience on June 24, 2020, Pope Francis explained how David helped teach us that there is one golden thread in life: prayer.

David teaches us to bring everything into dialogue with God: joy as guilt, love as suffering, friendship as much as an illness.

---

[3] Quoted in "Mother Teresa Quotes," *Spiritual Life*, accessed July 30, 2020, https://slife.org/mother-teresa-quotes/.

Everything can become a word addressed to the "You" who always listens to us.[4]

Prayer is our dialogue with God. We keep returning to Him, asking for His guidance, no matter our circumstances. And as the pope stated, this kind of humility helps prepare us to be open to what God is trying to say.

Prayer "is able to ensure the relationship with God, who is the true Companion of man's journey, in the midst of the many hardships of life: good or bad.... But always prayer: 'Thank you, Lord. I'm afraid, Lord. Help me, Lord. Forgive me, Lord.'"[5] So, as Elsa of *Frozen* fame would say: "Let it go." Better yet, as St. Paul reminds us, Jesus didn't exactly sit around and wait for us to get our proverbial act together. Instead, "while we were yet sinners Christ died for us" (Rom. 5:8).

On the opposite end of the spectrum is that awfully familiar age-old sin that first popped up in the Garden of Eden and led to the Fall: pride. The Old Testament book of Ecclesiastes tells us that "there is nothing new under the sun" (1:9). In other words, we're still struggling with the same major identity crisis experienced by Adam and Eve. We fall for the lie that we can be like God. We are not willing to recognize who God is and who we are not. As a result, we think we know what's best for us and proceed to tell the Creator of the universe, the Alpha and Omega, the Beginning and the End, that we've got this, and if He would just put a nice big rubber stamp of approval on our plans, everything will be just fine and dandy.

---

[4] Hannah Brockhaus, "Pope Francis: In life's ups and downs, make prayer your constant," Catholic News Agency, June 24, 2020, https://www.catholicnewsagency.com/news/pope-francis-in-lifes-ups-and-downs-make-prayer-your-constant-94851.

[5] Ibid.

That's how I lived a good portion of my life. Although I was raised Catholic and had a powerful experience when I made my First Holy Communion, the pull of the world was too strong for me to resist. When I was as young as eight or nine, God placed a love for communications on my heart. Both the religious and lay teachers at my Catholic grade school encouraged me to pursue media as my vocation, and I was off to the races, leaving God and my Faith in the rearview mirror. As I grew older, I still identified as Catholic, but my Faith didn't mean much to me beyond the weekly Mass obligation. Later on, even that fell by the wayside as I allowed myself to be completely consumed by a very demanding career as a broadcast journalist. Long story short, it took some very painful and dramatic events in my life to wake me up. The suffering brought me to my knees, but it also eventually brought me back to Christ and the Church.

My slow journey home to Rome began in the early nineties. While there was a great deal of pressure at that time for women to sacrifice everything for the job and the almighty dollar, the cultural influence is much stronger today. Catholics, as exemplified by my poor choices, are hardly immune: in fact, quite the opposite. We succumb to these influences all too often. More and more surveys reveal how self-identified Catholics do not necessarily take God and their Faith seriously. One very revealing survey released before the 2020 presidential election showed only about one in five Catholics said they believe in all of the Church's teachings:

> Overall, the poll found that 18% of Catholics indicate that they accept all of the Church's teachings and those are reflected in how they live their lives. An additional 38% report that they accept most teachings and try to live their lives accordingly; 29% do not accept some of the key teachings; 13% say Catholicism has only a minor influence on their lives; and 2% consider themselves former Catholics.

That relatively small group of Catholics often described as devout or active, one-fifth of the Catholic population, claims to accept all the teachings of the Church and lives and votes very differently from many of their fellow Americans and even their fellow Catholics. They are more active in their daily practice of the faith, go to Mass more often, and are guided by Catholic teaching on a more regular basis as they discern how to vote and how to respond to the great social issues and moral crises of our time. [6]

That 18 percent figure is startling. We are going our own way, doing our own thing. No wonder we are not hearing from God on a regular basis.

As you read through the incredible stories from our contributors, you will notice a similar theme. Quite a few of our authors had their own come-to-Jesus moments. It is said that pride comes before the fall. When we're talking about hearing from God, that fall turns out to be a blessing in disguise, because it forces us to fall on our knees. And that is when the real godly conversation begins.

I also hope you'll take notice of the variety of people represented on the following pages. God is constantly reaching out to all of us. He doesn't just speak to Catholic authors and speakers such as Al Kresta, Steve Ray, Kelly Wahlquist, and yours truly. In this book, you'll hear from a stay-at-home mom of five; an artist; a pro-life volunteer; a married couple who came close to divorce; a mom whose daughter struggled for years with epilepsy; a high school teacher; a marketing executive making her way into the Catholic Church; and many more people who at some point opened themselves up

[6] Matthew Bunson, "EWTN News/RealClear Opinion Research Poll No. 2: Finding the Catholic Vote," *National Catholic Register*, February 24, 2020, https://www.ncregister.com/daily-news/ewtn-news-realclear-opinion-research-poll-no.-2-finding-the-catholic-vote.

to hearing from God. Some, as you will read, already had a deep devotion to Christ and the Catholic Faith. Others cried out in sheer desperation, not even really knowing if God would answer, because they weren't quite sure God was even there.

My hope is that you'll see yourself in one or more of these wonderful brothers and sisters willing to bare their souls, quite literally, for nothing more than the desire to help you understand that God is not as far away as you might think. And, with a little effort, you will not only be able to hear from Him, but eventually will be chatting away with the Creator of the universe on a regular basis.

Seeking God through the Sounds of Silence

BY TERESA TOMEO

WORDS OF WISDOM

Remember that, as a friend of mine says, God answers "knee-mail"—but you won't hear those answers to prayer unless you spend less time with media and more time with God.

SAINTLY ADVICE

"We need to find God and He cannot be found in noise and restlessness. God is the friend of silence. See how nature, trees, flowers, grass grows in silence. See the stars the moon, the sun how they move in silence. We need silence to be able to touch souls." (Mother Teresa)

TERESA TOMEO is an author, syndicated Catholic talk-show host, and motivational speaker with more than thirty years of experience in TV, radio and newspaper. She spent nineteen of those years working in front of a camera as a reporter and anchor in the Detroit market. In 2000, Teresa left the secular media to start her own speaking and communications company, Teresa Tomeo Communications, LLC and her website and blog (TeresaTomeo. com). Her daily morning radio program, *Catholic Connection*, is produced by Ave Maria Radio and EWTN's Global Catholic Radio Network and can be heard on over five hundred domestic and international AM and FM radio affiliates worldwide, including SiriusXM Satellite Radio. Over the past two decades, Teresa has traveled extensively throughout Italy and has led pilgrimages and tours there more than fifty times. In 2019, she founded T's Italy, a travel consultation company, along with its website (TravelItaly-Expert.com), where she shares insider tips for where to eat, stay, shop and play in this beautiful country. Following the outbreak of COVID-19, Teresa published *Conquering Coronavirus: How Faith Can Put Your Fears to Rest*. Teresa also began a positivity movement to encourage listeners and followers to stay focused on the true, the beautiful, and the good. This includes T's Teatime: A Cup of Inspiration to Warm Your Heart and Soul (TeresaTomeo.com/ inspiration), where she shares inspirational videos and uplifting social media messaging to help others embrace a deeper joy that is not dependent on one's circumstances, but on the many gifts that God has given. Teresa's next book, *The Joy of Positive Thinking*, is expected to be released by Sophia Institute Press in 2021. To learn about more future books by Teresa published by Sophia Institute Press, please visit www.sophiainstitute.com/author/teresa-tomeo.

I love what Mother Teresa has to say about silence, especially the last line concerning our need for silence to touch souls. Silence was something she spoke of often when asked by her fellow sisters, among others, on how to get closer to God. Her reference to touching souls, I firmly believe, pertains not only to how silence allows us to touch the souls of others, but also to how it allows us to let God touch our own souls first. So, with the words of a great and recently canonized Catholic saint in mind, if you're having trouble hearing from God, take a good, honest look at the level of noise in your life.

As I discovered when I began to have my many much-needed come-to-Jesus moments, my noise levels were a lot higher than I realized. This was a double whammy for me. Not only was I giving way too much attention and importance to what the mass media and our culture in general were saying, but I worked in the very arena that was churning out those deceiving messages 24/7. My job as a broadcast journalist required me to be closely connected to TV, newspaper, and radio outlets. Obviously, it was important for me to be aware of local happenings and developments, but I took it way too far. It was so easy to convince myself that it was crucial to be almost literally tethered to all forms of communication. And this was back in the eighties and nineties, before e-mail and cell phones, not to mention the all-too-consuming social media streams, came on the scene in full force. For me, being connected meant turning on the radio as soon as I woke up and then watching the local TV news channels before I headed out the door. Once in the car, I would immediately continue listening to nonstop chatter about the happenings in the city and the world by tuning to the major news station on my way to work. With the noise in the car and my long drive in a major metropolitan area, even the slightest hint of silence would be afraid to show up anywhere near my neck of the woods.

The pattern would continue when I arrived home in the evening. The amount of time I spent monitoring every news outlet in town was unnecessary, and my obsession with always being in the know was consuming practically every waking minute of my day. I suffered from a severe case of FOMO—"fear of missing out." Once cell phones and laptops became common, it got even worse.

In addition to all this noise, there was this loud voice (more like voices) in my head: the constant messages drilled into me in journalism school, internships, and newsrooms. This is what it took to be successful. The career came first, and my career meant all media, all the time. There was no room for anything or anyone else, including God and my husband. It took a crisis in my marriage and my career for me to wake up, smell the cappuccino, and start paying attention to more than just the news. It wasn't easy to go through what I refer to as my "cultural detox." But gradually, as I made my way back to the Church, I learned to incorporate more silence and less noise. It didn't mean giving up all media all the time. It meant finding balance and starting the day with God in the daily Mass readings instead of the local or national news. That's a healthy habit that my husband and I still practice almost daily. We take time to do the readings together and briefly discuss them before beginning the busyness of the day.

Recent studies show that adults are surrounded by all sorts of noise during practically every waking hour. And these studies aren't including the noise that fills our lives that isn't media-related: horns honking, people talking, dogs barking, alarms ringing, and so on. A 2018 study conducted by Nielsen found that adults in the United

States spend over eleven hours a day connected to some sort of media.[7] This is not just an American phenomenon: shortly after Italy was forced into lockdown in March 2020, Pope Francis expressed his fear that Italian families would turn into households of monks, but not in a good way. In an interview with *La Repubblica*, the pope said he was very concerned that Italians would grow further apart during their time behind closed doors because they were more closely connected to the virtual world than to each other and to God:

> Sometimes, we only experience a virtual form of communication with one another. Instead, we should discover a new closeness. More concrete relationships made of attention and patience. In their homes, families often eat together in great silence, but not as a result of listening to each other, rather because the parents watch television while they eat, and children are on their mobile phones. They look like monks, all isolated from each other. Here there is no communication, whereas listening to each other is important because that's how we can understand the needs, efforts, desires of the other. This language made of concrete gestures must be safeguarded.[8]

Notice how our contributors, while all having different backgrounds and experiences, often heard from God either in a period of silence or following time alone in prayer. It may not have been the

---

[7] "Time Flies: U.S. Adults Now Spend Nearly Half a Day Interacting with Media," Nielsen, July 31, 2018, https://www.nielsen.com/us/en/insights/article/2018/time-flies-us-adults-now-spend-nearly-half-a-day-interacting-with-media/.

[8] Pope Francis, "Pope Francis on Coronavirus crisis: 'Don't waste these difficult days. While at home re-discover the importance of hugging kids and relatives,'" interview by Paolo Rodari, *La Repubblica*, March 18, 2020, https://www.repubblica.it/vaticano/2020/03/18/news/coronavirus_pope_francis-251572693/.

most sophisticated prayer. But they asked and they heard because, at some point, they were able to rise above the noise.

And since God is God, there's no denying He can get our attention in the midst of a busy, noisy world. In Scripture, He often comes to us, as Mother Teresa reminds us, in silence, or, if not complete silence, something pretty close to it.

And he [the Lord] said, "Go forth, and stand upon the mount before the Lord." And behold, the Lord passed by, and a great and strong wind tore the mountains, and broke in pieces the rocks before the Lord, but the Lord was not in the wind; and after the wind an earthquake, but the Lord was not in the earthquake; and after the earthquake a fire, but the Lord was not in the fire; and after the fire a still small voice. (1 Kings 19:11–12)

As you begin to read the following testimonies, turn off the TV, mute that cell phone, and surround yourself with nothing but the peaceful sounds of silence. See how God speaks. He may at this moment be trying to speak to you as well.

REFLECTIONS

———

FROM SCRIPTURE

*"Rising very early before dawn,
he [Jesus] left and went off to a
deserted place, where he prayed."
(Mark 1:35, NABRE)*

———

QUESTIONS

What type of noise do you think
keeps you from hearing God?

How much time each day do you spend
on media that may be preventing you
from experiencing Godcidences?

Do you have a favorite quiet place
where you can pray, reflect, read, and
retreat from the noise of the world?

How often do you read and
reflect upon Scripture?

Angel at the Train Station

BY TERESA TOMEO

WORDS OF WISDOM

God loves us so much that He provides for us in all sorts of surprising and unexpected ways, including through His angels.

SAINTLY ADVICE

"God is humanity's universal teacher and guardian, but his teaching to humanity is mediated by angels." (St. Thomas Aquinas)

My husband, Dominick, and I were proud of ourselves. We had navigated four of the five towns along Italy's beautiful Ligurian coast quite well. It had been a picture-perfect day in the magical and colorful region known as Cinque Terre ("five lands"). It was September 2008, and we were celebrating our twenty-fifth anniversary, wrapping up the experience at a waterfront restaurant in Vernazza. As we raised yet another glass of prosecco, we marveled at how smooth our experience had been. We began by hopping on the well-known Cinque Terre Express near where we were staying in lovely Rapallo. The train is the best way to travel (unless you take a boat), as the five villages are not reachable by car. The other way to get through Cinque Terre and to take in the beauty of both the mountains and the sea is via what is referred to in Italy as the St. Francis donkey, more commonly known as your own two feet. We did a combination of train and trek, so to speak.

So off we went at about nine in the morning from our hotel to the train station, ready to hit the Cinque Terre hiking trail. We stepped off the train in the southernmost town, charming Riomaggiore, and spent the day heading north toward Vernazza and Monterosso, taking our time to stop and immerse ourselves for a few hours in as many of the quaint towns as possible. Of course, being in Italy meant grabbing a panino and a glass of vino or two along the way. The Cinque Terre trail connecting all the villages is about seven miles long, winding through the mountains high above the sea. The spectacular views give you a chance to get a real appreciation for the beauty of the northeast Italian coastline.

We were hoping to finish up dinner in time to stop in Monterosso before heading back to our hotel for the evening, but our restaurant was so lovely we couldn't tear ourselves away from the sounds and the sunset along the water, not to mention the fantastic food and the lively atmosphere of an Italian fishing village. Sounds cliché, I know, but I felt as if I had stepped into a painting.

Before we knew it, it was closing in on ten o'clock. Although we had plenty of time, since the train ran along the coast until one in the morning, we thought it would be a good idea to get back to the hotel, as we had to hit the road and head to Lake Como early the next morning.

We hopped backed on the train, expecting smooth sailing again. The railcars were practically empty, and we continued reminiscing about our incredible day in Cinque Terre. We thanked God for the experience and for blessing us with twenty-five years together, especially since, at one point, we thought we were going to end up in divorce court. We were so joyful and grateful at the same time. Little did we know our travel bubble would begin to burst, big-time, in only a few minutes. We were moving along, looking out at the night sky, when suddenly, instead of passing through one of the small stations as we did that morning, we came to a complete stop. Someone said very loudly, "Andiamo," or "Let's go." We were being told to exit the train ASAP. This did not make any sense. With the little Italian we knew, we tried awfully hard to explain to the ticket collector that we were heading to Rapallo, so surely, he didn't mean us. We even pointed to our tickets, but nothing we said (or tried to say) mattered. The handful of passengers on the train had to exit stage left.

So now what? The tiny station was almost completely dark, except for one lone streetlamp outside the ticket office. The few people who were on the train had all gone their separate ways to who knew where, since we were in the middle of the mountains, already several miles from Vernazza and another twenty miles or so to Rapallo. There was no cell phone service and as far as we could see—and we looked all around—not a soul to be found. We did notice a long bench on the other side of the platform and joked about resting there until the next train or the sunrise, whichever came first. We could not imagine leaving the station as there were no signs of any other villages in sight. We both agreed we would have to stay put at least for a bit to see if anyone showed up. If not, we would start walking somewhere, anywhere that at least had cell service.

We did not have to wait very long, as suddenly, out of the corner of my eye, I noticed a man standing about ten feet to my right dressed in some sort of uniform. He was wearing a crisp white shirt and blue pants and appeared to be a police officer or maybe a conductor. He had a cap under one arm and looked very official, but I had no idea where he came from. He seemed to appear out of nowhere, and when I first glanced at him, he had his head down and was looking at his phone. We did not notice him on the train earlier, and when we stepped off, we were very quickly by ourselves, or so we thought. As I was about to take a step toward him to ask some questions, he turned to me. He began to speak to me in English, with an Italian accent. Normally, since my husband and I are both of Italian heritage and look every bit the part, most Italians begin the conversation in their native language. But not this time. As he was speaking, all sorts of questions were running through my mind. How did he know we're American or from an English-speaking country? Did he hear us talking a few minutes ago? But how could that be, since we'd been by ourselves?

"If you're heading back to Rapallo, get back on the same train," he said, pointing to where we had exited earlier. "Wait about fifteen minutes and you'll be on your way."

Again, more questions were running through my mind. How did he know we were on that train? How did he know we were going to

Rapallo? And how was it possible that the train would start up again when the entire area seemed so deserted?

"Don't worry," he said, smiling. "You'll be fine. That train is heading back to Rapallo. All you have to do is wait a while."

"Grazie," said my husband and I, and we began to walk back to the train. I turned around to thank him one more time for his reassurance and directions, but he was gone. Now, that just did not seem possible. We had barely taken a few steps, and we hadn't heard or noticed any type of movement, so we expected to see him still there, looking at his phone.

We rode the train back in silence for the most part, trying to understand what had happened. On our way to Lake Como, we discussed the possibility that God sent us an angel to help us get back home.

We kept the story pretty much to ourselves, sharing it with only a few close friends. However, not too long ago, I was interviewing a priest, Fr. John Horgan, who wrote the wonderful book *His Angels at Our Side: Understanding Their Power in Our Souls and the World.* During a commercial break, I asked him if I could speak with him about our experience in Cinque Terre when we resumed the on-air discussion. He was very gracious and proceeded to tell me that the man could very possibly have been an angel. He even went so far as to say that his providential appearance was a blessing or a gift from God for our anniversary, in recognition of the joy and the gratitude we were feeling.

That was a tough interview to finish, as my emotions almost got the better of me. I believe deep down Dominick and I both knew something extraordinary had happened. Having such validation from a holy and knowledgeable priest was the icing on the cake.

REFLECTIONS

——

FROM SCRIPTURE

*"For he will give his angels charge of you
to guard you in all your ways." (Psalm 91:11)*

——

QUESTIONS

How much do you know about angels?

How have you learned about angels—from
our culture or from the Church?

Do you think you may have
encountered an angel?

Are you willing to share that experience
with others in order to encourage
someone struggling in his walk of faith?

Coincidental Evangelizing

BY PATTI MAGUIRE ARMSTRONG

WORDS OF WISDOM

Even though we may not always receive an immediate response to our petitions, God is very much with us and hears our every prayer. When we offer our lives in service of Him, He will take us up on that offer and lead the way. Walking with the Lord means having a strong prayer life and trusting in Him. It is when we experience coincidences that we feel His presence.

SAINTLY ADVICE

"The greater and more persistent your confidence in God, the more abundantly you will receive all that you ask." (St. Albert the Great)

PATTI MAGUIRE ARMSTRONG is an award-winning author and blogger at the *National Catholic Register* and was the managing editor and co-author of Ascension Press's best-selling Amazing Grace series. Her newest books are *Holy Hacks: Everyday Ways to Live Your Faith and Get to Heaven* and *Big Hearted: Inspiring Stories from Everyday Families*. She has a bachelor's in social work and a master's in public administration, and worked in both those fields before staying home to work as a freelance writer. Patti and her husband, Mark, live in North Dakota, where they raised ten children, two of whom were AIDS orphans from Kenya. Follow her on Twitter @PattiArmstrong and read her blog at PattiMaguireArmstrong.com or at the *National Catholic Register*.

After I began saying the Rosary over thirty years ago, I started to see God's hand in events not as a coincidence, but as His personal interaction with us. A book about Marian apparitions had inspired me to pray the Rosary daily. But one night in the spring of 1990, I was so tired, I thought, "There's no way I can stay awake and pray a Rosary tonight."

At that very moment, I heard a book fall from the bookshelf onto the bed. I had been facing the other way. Before turning to look, I thought to myself, "Watch it be the Bible, and I'll end up feeling guilty for not praying the Rosary." Instead, it was the very book with the Blessed Mother's picture on the cover that had originally inspired me to pray the Rosary.

"Wow, that's a big coincidence," I thought. I found the energy to pray the Rosary that night.

This same scenario occurred a few days later: I had not prayed my Rosary yet, and I was so tired. I had just gotten our newborn son to sleep. "There is no possible way I can stay up to say a Rosary," I thought. At that very moment, I saw with my own eyes the same book tumble from the bookshelf onto the bed. It again landed with the Blessed Mother's picture faceup.

I held my breath in awe. I was not even moving when the book fell. I realized it was no coincidence that at the exact moment I decided not to pray the Rosary, the book that had inspired me to pray it fell off the shelf with the Blessed Mother's picture facing me. God knew my thoughts. And He knew how to get my attention at just the right time.

Since then, I have discovered ways to work in union with God's coincidences. For those not walking with Our Lord, coincidences are a marvel. People gush, "What are the odds?" But as Christians who walk with the Lord, we are not amazed at the odds; we are amazed at God.

One of the ways that I have actually opened up the door to coincidences is through asking for them in order to evangelize casually. Before taking a seat on a plane or at an event, I send up a prayer: "God, you decide whom I sit next to and direct our conversation." That's it. Many times, the person sitting next to me has said, "It must have been meant to be that you sat next to me."

Then, the person really looks surprised when I say: "I believe so. I asked God to decide who I sat next to and to direct our conversation." It does not happen every single time, but it does happen very often, especially on planes, since I fly periodically to visit family or for some work-related trip. I actually know a couple of other people who do the same thing, with the same results.

It is probably safe to say that most Catholics are uncomfortable sharing their Faith. We are commanded, however, to go out and spread the good news. The *Catechism of the Catholic Church* says: "Baptism, Confirmation, and Eucharist are sacraments of Christian initiation. They ground the common vocation of all Christ's disciples, a vocation to holiness and to the mission of evangelizing the world" (CCC 1533). And Christ told the apostles, "Go therefore and make disciples of all nations, baptizing them in the name of the Father and of the Son and of the Holy Spirit, teaching them to observe all that I have commanded you" (Matt. 28:19).

By praying, "God, you decide whom I sit next to and direct our conversation," I simply volunteer for duty and let God lead the way. The first time I said this prayer was before flying home to visit my parents. At one of the stops along the way, the plane was grounded for a time while some maintenance issue was tended to. A conversation with my seatmate, who worked for public TV in the children's division, began with a bit of small talk. From there, he shared about a dilemma he and his wife were having with their two daughters.

"You need to pray about it," I said, which led to his admission that he didn't pray anymore, which led to a deeper conversation about faith. Our discussion had clearly affected him.

"My wife is not going to believe this conversation we had when I tell her," he told me at the end. "She knows that I never talk to anyone on planes."

Another time, I was flying back from EWTN after being interviewed about *Amazing Grace for Mothers* on the *Bookmark* program. The nursing student next to me was returning home from a weekend visiting her husband, who was training to be a pilot. Her in-laws were babysitting their two children. She talked at length about a lot of things. Toward the end of the flight, she asked if I had any children.

"Yes, I have eight," I said (our last two came later).

She threw herself to the side of her seat and looked me up and down.

"You don't look religious," she stammered. Then, she took a breath and asked: "Eight? How can you do that? Doesn't it get to you at times?"

At that point, the Holy Spirit gave me words I had never even thought of before.

"Flight attendants are thought to have glamorous lives, aren't they?" I asked.

"Yes."

I pointed to the flight attendant in front of us putting trash in a black garbage bag. "What is she doing?"

"Cleaning up."

"And you are studying to be a nurse, right?"

"Yes."

"Will you be emptying bedpans and taking care of sick patients?"

"Yes."

"I'll tell you the difference between that and what I do," I said. "When I take care of my children, I am taking care of the people I love most in the world. So how is anything better than that?"

She looked stunned.

"I think I was supposed to sit next to you," she said.

I have no idea what was going on in her life to make what I said strike her so deeply, but I've witnessed this kind of reaction many times.

God has seated me next to fallen-away Catholics and people struggling to have any faith at all. Once, I sat next to a woman who shared with me about a friend of hers who was unable to get past the deaths of both of her children five years earlier. I told her about Deb Hadley, a speaker with some beautiful videos, who had lost both of her children as well.

"This is an answer to prayer!" the woman told me. "It must have been meant to be that you sat next to me."

The constant repetition of this sentence alone is a coincidence beyond odds. If someone offered me a million dollars to get my seatmate to say that exact sentence, it's unlikely that I would be able to collect that money. Yet to hear it so often after I say my prayer is evidence that God is happy to conspire with us to create coincidences for His glory and His love for us.

REFLECTIONS

———

FROM SCRIPTURE

"And I will walk among you and will be your God, and you shall be my people." (Leviticus 26:12)

"So, whether you eat or drink, or whatever you do, do all to the glory of God." (1 Corinthians 10:31)

"Again Jesus spoke to them, saying, 'I am the light of the world; he who follows me will not walk in darkness, but will have the light of life.'" (John 8:12)

———

QUESTIONS

What are some of the ways you can open doors to God in your life?

Can you think of experiences you
initially thought to be coincidences,
only to realize that God was working
with you on something?

Have you encountered people
whom you now realize were being
led by God to work in your life?

Lady in White

BY TERESA TOMEO

WORDS OF WISDOM

Don't doubt the possibility of your own angel encounter.

SAINTLY ADVICE

*"The first thing about the angels that we
ought to imitate is their consciousness of the
Presence of God." (St. John Vianney)*

It had been a while since I thought about an amazing encounter that my parents had shortly after I was born. The story of that encounter came rushing back a few days before my mom died on the feast of St. Joseph, March 19, 2020. Two days before her death, she rallied a bit and was talking with me. I am not sure if she realized she was dying or understood she was in hospice care. But she was lucid enough to ask me some questions, including the questions that gave me chills and reminded me of the storied lady in white.

As I was giving my mom some chicken soup, she looked up at me and asked, "Where did they go?"

"Where did who go, Mom? There's no one else here," I said.

"The people who were praying at the door earlier. They were standing in the doorway a little while ago praying, and they're not there anymore."

My mom was very adamant that there were people praying for her in the doorway of her assisted-living apartment. My sister and I had been there all day for several days and had been visited only by social workers, the hospice nurse, and other living relatives. Did she see my late father, who died in 2010, or perhaps my other sister, Donna, who died in 2016? It could have been any one of her many deceased loved ones, including her own parents and siblings. I had no doubt that my mom was experiencing something similar to her mysterious meeting shortly after I was born. It may sound like something out of a fictional ghost story, but just speak with anyone who works in geriatrics or who cares for the dying. Too many coincidences—or, again, Godcidences—to ignore what those in the final stages of life are hearing and seeing.

I first heard about the lady in white when I was in grade school. I was always very inquisitive and wanted to know all the details surrounding my birthday. While my parents were thrilled when baby number three, yours truly, came along, the story of my birth was not all sunshine and roses. Mom was rushed to the hospital for heavy bleeding. Although my birth itself was relatively normal, Mom started having all sorts of pain once she returned home. My parents had barely placed me in the crib when Mom was whisked away in an ambulance. Apparently, her uterus had been damaged during the delivery, and the bleeding was so severe that she needed immediate surgery. Mom said she never saw my father so petrified.

As my parents waited nervously for more information about the procedure from the medical staff, a young woman approached them. The visitor had very dark hair, which contrasted starkly with her sparkling white uniform. The minute the young woman smiled at her, Mom felt a sense of peace come over her immediately, as did Dad. My parents were not sure if the woman was a nurse or a volunteer. But they remember her kindness, her sincerity, and that beautiful smile. She put them right at ease. Even though she was only with them for a few short minutes, they felt very protected and comforted by her presence. As the medical staff were about to wheel my mom away to prep for the surgery, the lady in white leaned over and squeezed my mom's hand—the hand that was holding a rosary—and said, "Don't worry, everything is going to be okay, and you're going to be fine."

Everything was okay, and Mom was fine. There was only one problem. My parents were never able to thank the young woman. They told the nurses and doctors about their encounter and how they wanted to express gratitude for her support. The staff insisted none of the nurses or volunteers fit that description. They had no idea of whom Mom was speaking.

My parents believe the lady in white was real. Every time they shared the story, they remembered every detail. Most importantly, they remember the comfort and reassurance they felt as soon as she showed up. Mom and Dad were faithful Catholics and not given to inventing stories. They couldn't be absolutely sure, but all their lives, they wondered if perhaps God sent an angel to them at a time of great need.

And why not? After all, angels are indeed biblical: we read about them throughout the Old and New Testaments. They announced the birth of Jesus. The angel Gabriel greeted Mary with the good news of her role in salvation history. Angels ministered to Jesus in the Garden of Gethsemane and proclaimed the Resurrection to Mary Magdalene and the apostles. No wonder the saints and our Catholic teachings have so much to say about these creatures. In paragraphs 350 to 354 of the *Catechism*, we read that angels are spiritual creatures who, among other things, "glorify God without ceasing and who serve his saving plans for other creatures" (CCC 350).

The *Catechism* goes on to say that angels exist to help the Church in her work here on earth:

> The angels surround Christ their Lord. They serve him especially in the accomplishment of his saving mission to men. The Church venerates the angels who help her on her earthly pilgrimage and protect every human being. God willed the diversity of his creatures and their own particular goodness, their interdependence and their order. He destined all material creatures for the good of the human race. Man, and through him all creation, is destined for the glory of God. Respect for laws inscribed in creation and the relations which derive from the nature of things is a principle of wisdom and a foundation for morality. (CCC 351-354)

A beautiful prayer about angels is attributed to the great St. Augustine:

> Watch, O Lord, with those who wake, or watch or weep to-night, and give your angels charge over those who sleep. Tend your sick ones, O Lord Jesus Christ; rest your weary ones; bless your dying ones; soothe your suffering ones; pity your afflicted ones; shield your joyous ones; and all for your love's sake. Amen.[9]

Perhaps the lady in white who tended to Mom when she was sick returned at the end of Mom's life to bless her as she was dying and, as Hebrews 1:14 reminds us, to minister to her as she was about to inherit her salvation.

[9]   Posted at AZ Quotes, accessed July 31, 2020, https://www.azquotes.com/quote/393163.

REFLECTIONS

———

FROM SCRIPTURE

"Are not all angels ministering spirits sent to serve those who will inherit salvation?" (Hebrews 1:14, NIV)

———

QUESTIONS

How does the knowledge that angels exist and are active in our lives comfort you?

Why do you think Scripture makes so many references to angels?

Do you have a favorite angel story in the Bible? If so, which one and why?

Pre-prayed Delivery

BY KAITLYN CURTIN

WORDS OF WISDOM

Christ was born in Bethlehem before, not because, we turned to Him with all our hearts. That same unearned grace made a special delivery for me.

SAINTLY ADVICE

"Receive Communion often, very often.... There you have the sole remedy, if you want to be cured. Jesus has not put this attraction in your heart for nothing." (St. Thérèse of Lisieux)

KAITLYN CURTIN holds master's degrees in theological studies and in education from the University of Notre Dame. She has taught theology courses at many levels and in many settings—high school, college, adult distance education, catechist certification, parish religious education, and homeschool. In addition to raising her five children to the light, she assists religion teachers with professional development through presentations and consulting. You can connect with her on Facebook at https://www.facebook.com/kdcurtin.

Can paperwork count as prayer?

On the hospital preregistration form, I had listed my religion as Roman Catholic and checked yes to chaplain visits. It didn't occur to me as I handed in the form and payment that I was now not only prepaid: I was pre-prayed.

For baby number five, the doctor had ordered another induction. Ugh. Induction contractions are unnatural and horrible, and I was averse to anesthesia because of past experiences. Why waste such exquisite suffering? I intended to offer up my labor pains for the conversion and salvation of a relative. I had tried this with four births, each time managing not to pray at all once the agony started. This time would be different! I would actually pray! I would suffer for a noble cause with a good attitude!

Two hours into the induction, I wasn't "tolerating the pain" very well, which is hospital-speak for "the patient is swearing at the people helping her." Once again, my grand gesture of offering up my labor wasn't really happening; that spiritual hundred-dollar gift card was rapidly depreciating to zero.

Five hours into the induction, my doctor finally came on shift, and I looked forward to hearing that I was at least progressing. Unfortunately, he discovered, all that pain had come without progress, and worse, my nine-pound son was stretched out sideways. He had been in a perfect position in the ultrasound images just a few days before. How could this have happened?

Two weeks later, the doctor would admit that the nurse made a medical mistake by not confirming the baby's presentation before starting the induction. I had never been informed that Pitocin, once started, makes delivery a now-or-never event. At this point, options were very limited: if I wanted, the doctor could apply great pressure in an attempt to manipulate the baby out of his transverse position, but it would hurt like crazy, would not work, and would waste time, and then I would need an emergency C-section anyway. He suggested we skip to the inevitable C-section.

Not ready to give up on my plan, I asked him to try physical manipulation. The doctor was not pleased.

"Sign your anesthesia consent while the Pitocin gets out of your system," he said. "I'll be back in thirty minutes."

My mother and my husband were trying to help me find calm and make a new plan as I ranted between contractions about how this wasn't fair. I was angry, confused, and panicked. I thought of the baby I had miscarried a few years before. Was I was going to lose this one, too? Right then, I should have prayed and asked for divine assistance. But I didn't. Jesus came anyway.

Literally, Jesus came in the room just then. A tall, beautiful woman holding a pyx walked in and simply said, "Would anyone like to receive?"

This is humiliating to admit, but my first thought was about the rules: "I'm not allowed to eat during labor. You shouldn't be here asking me this. We didn't send for you. Are you even allowed to visit women in active labor?"

My second thought was, "YES."

"The Body of Christ."

"Amen."

The baby flipped into position the second the host was on my tongue. I felt him do it. God wanted to make sure the connection was obvious to me. My enormous baby son instantly did exactly what he needed to do for a healthy birth. The sensation was unlike anything I had ever experienced during pregnancy. I bet this is what John did to Elizabeth when Mary visited with Jesus in her womb.

The doctor returned, and I told him that the baby had moved. With a patronizing smile, he told me to lie down for a check. He was in disbelief.

"What did you do?" he asked.

"She received Communion!" yelled my mom.

"It's a Eucharistic miracle!" my husband declared.

In the Gospel, when Jesus healed Peter's mother-in-law, she immediately got up and went to work. In the delivery ward, the miraculous flip was not the end of my work. The afternoon included my capitulation to an epidural, as I went from half to fully dilated in one hour. Daniel was born with strange lesions that required a biopsy (but turned out to be innocuous), and I endured a major illness two weeks later. God's intervention was no promise of perpetual health, or even (as pandemic days have shown) a guarantee of future Communions. Yet the Divine Physician acted in a way that utterly exceeded the quality and timing of my prayer. I couldn't offer up my labor for a soul in need, and I couldn't pray when I was in pain, but God reminded me that it is not about what I can do or what I have earned. It is about what His love makes possible. He is really and truly present, and the initiative is His.

Blessed be Jesus in the Most Holy Sacrament of the Altar.

REFLECTIONS

———

FROM SCRIPTURE

"One generation praises your deeds to the next
and proclaims your mighty works."
(Psalm 145:4, NABRE)

"Jesus said to them, 'Amen, amen, I
say to you, unless you eat the flesh
of the Son of Man and drink his
blood, you do not have life within
you.'" (John 6:53, NABRE)

———

QUESTIONS

When have you waited for a
difficulty to peak before you truly
turned to God in prayer?

When has pain or grief caused
you to have trouble praying?

Could you feel God holding
you in those times?

What difficulties can you expect
to encounter in the near future,
and in what ways can you pray
ahead of future suffering?

The chaplain who gave me the Eucharist
really lived out her call to ministry,
going boldly into a ward where she
might have been less than welcome. She
came right to the point, asking, "Can I
share Jesus with you?" Who in your life
brings you Jesus in difficult moments?

Can you overcome awkwardness to
do the same for those around you in
such a direct and beautiful way?

Give Us This Bread Always!

BY KELLY WAHLQUIST

WORDS OF WISDOM

Signs, signs, signs—everywhere, God gives us signs. God created us for Himself, and as such, He uses every time and every place to draw close to us. The more we seek to know and love Him, the more He will make us aware of His presence in our lives, and many times He does this through signs—sometimes subtle, sometimes not so subtle.

SAINTLY ADVICE

"God thirsts that we would thirst for him." (St. Augustine)

KELLY WAHLQUIST is a Catholic speaker and author. She is the founder of WINE: Women in the New Evangelization, and director of the Archbishop Flynn Catechetical Institute. She's the author of *Created to Relate: God's Design for Peace & Joy*, and her latest books, *Walk in Her Sandals* and *Gaze Upon Jesus*, are innovative, collaborative works that allow women to relate to Jesus the way they were created to—as women. Find Kelly at CatholicVineyard.com.

The moment I saw the subject line "Sacrament of Holy Communion Sign Up" in my inbox, I opened the e-mail and signed up for the first available time slot! After six weeks of not being able to receive the Eucharist due to the pandemic lockdown, my heart yearned to receive the Body, Blood, Soul, and Divinity of Jesus, and I ached for the graces that come with the sacrament. For the week leading up to Tuesday, April 28, I anticipated being reunited with my Lord like a child anticipating Christmas morning. On Sunday, as I made my spiritual communion while "going to Mass" on my laptop in my living room, I was greatly comforted knowing I would be receiving Jesus in Communion in just forty-eight hours. Thirty-six hours later, my solace shattered.

After a five-mile run Monday evening, I plopped down on my bed, iPhone in hand, and listened to the messages on my voicemail. The first message was from my pastor, telling me he was sorry, but due to an overscheduling of people, he had to reschedule my time to receive my Lord and Savior. My heart sank. I knew it wasn't my pastor's fault, but I had waited so long and yearned so deeply.

"Jesus, what are you doing?" I asked. "I want to be with you!"

Devastated, I called a friend, who instantly restored my peace by letting me know that her parish had daily Adoration beginning at seven in the morning (for ten or fewer people at a time). Well, if I couldn't receive Jesus in the Eucharist, I would sit with Him a while in the Blessed Sacrament.

When my alarm went off at five-thirty, I eagerly jumped out of bed (something I hadn't done at all during the stay-at-home order!).

And, as this was a big day, I opted to forego the sweatpants I'd been living in and donned a nice pair of pants, with a real button and zipper. Luckily, they fit! I did my best to cover the Bonnie Raitt gray streak, compliments of quarantine, and raced out of the house. I wanted to make sure I was one of the first ten people to the church—I needed to see Jesus!

I walked into the church five minutes early and was relieved to see only three other people. Praise God! I would get to be with my Lord! As I waited for the deacon to expose the Blessed Sacrament, I knelt and began to pray. Instantly, my mind, which had been on overload day and night for six weeks, quieted. Within moments, the deacon placed the monstrance with the Blessed Sacrament on the altar, and I had a sincere, tender, and loving conversation with the One I so desperately missed. My eyes were closed, but my heart was open. It felt as though I were in another world, blissfully immersed in the spiritual realm. For the first time in weeks, all of me—mind, body, and spirit—was still. Soon, the shuffling of feet interrupted my moment of calm. Looking up, I watched as my three co-adorers went up and knelt at the communion rail (six feet apart), and I saw the deacon descend the steps with the Eucharist.

"Can this be happening?" I thought. "Do I really get to receive my Lord and my God in the Eucharist?"

I made my way up to the communion rail, and taking my place six feet from my sister in Christ, I tearfully received Communion. I went back to my spot in the pew praising and giving thanks to the Lord for leading me to Him on this rainy morning. After a few more moments in prayer, I sat down, grabbed my iPhone, and looked up the Gospel of the day. I opened my Bible to John 6:30–34. I couldn't believe what I was reading!

"Are you kidding me, Lord?" I thought.

There, on the ever-highlighted and ever-underlined page of my Bible, was God speaking right to me in a new way. He was speaking to the anguish I had experienced in the past twelve hours, not to mention the past six weeks of being isolated from everyone, but most importantly from Him! Call it what you will—a Godcidence, a God-wink, or Jesus showing off—whatever you name it, it was my Lord speaking directly to me—the one who longed to see Him, the one who yearned to receive Him in the Eucharist.

I looked down at my Bible and read: "So they said to him, 'Then what sign do you do, that we may see, and believe you? What work do you perform?'" (John 6:30).

My heart answered: "Lord, you let me *see* you here today because you had bigger and better plans for me. I yearned to receive you in the Eucharist, and I settled (albeit an exceptional settling!) to sit with you in the church, but you *worked* it such that I had both, and you gave me yet another marvelous reason to *believe!*"

I continued reading. "Our fathers ate the manna in the wilderness; as it is written, 'He gave them bread from heaven to eat'" (John 6:31).

"Lord," I prayed, "you will never forsake me. You will not leave me orphaned in this crazy pandemic wilderness that has caused my mind to wander aimlessly and has brought doubt into my heart. You will always provide for my every need—I need to put my trust in you."

"Jesus then said to them, 'Truly, truly, I say to you, it was not Moses who gave you the bread from heaven; my Father gives you the true bread from heaven. For the bread of God is that which comes down from heaven, and gives life to the world'" (John 6:32-33).

My prayer: "Lord, I spend my life teaching others that God loves them and has an amazing plan for their lives. I share how sin interrupted that plan, but God, in His infinite mercy, sent His only Son, who, taking on human form, became one of us, walked among us, suffered with us, and died for us so that we might have eternal life. So often, I share that we have to reorient our lives to God because that's where we find our peace, our joy, our happiness. Lord, how did I let this pandemic put so much space between what my lips proclaim and what my heart believes?"

As my prayer continued, I heard in my heart, "You have been given this time to yearn for the Most Holy Sacrament that you might reorient your life to me, that you might truly believe in me, that you might put your trust in me and know that I am with you always." And, as crazy as it sounds, at this moment, the words of a Carole King song filled my mind. (For some reason, my prayers never involve Gregorian Chant!) I heard, "You just call out my name, and you know wherever I am, I'll come running ... to see you again."

As the corners of my mouth turned up, I thought: "He's right. All I have to do is call on Him, for He is there during every season of my life—winter, spring, summer, or fall." Then, I looked down and read the final verse of the Gospel reading: "Lord, give us this bread always" (John 6:34).

My heart smiled when I realized that as it turns out, I've got a friend, and He *is* the Bread of Life—and He is with me always!

REFLECTIONS

FROM SCRIPTURE

"Jesus said to them, 'I am the bread of life; he who comes to me shall not hunger, and he who believes in me shall never thirst.'" (John 6:35)

QUESTIONS

How has the coronavirus pandemic affected your relationship with God and His Church?

Have you come to appreciate the sacraments, especially the Eucharist, even more? How?

How much time do you spend in Eucharistic Adoration?

Are you willing to spend more time with the Lord in the Blessed Sacrament in order to grow even closer to Him?

The Bread of Angels
and a Hug from Heaven

BY TERESA TOMEO

WORDS OF WISDOM

*Even though we may not realize it, gratitude is a
form of prayer to which God loves to respond.*

SAINTLY ADVICE

*"When you have received Him, stir up your heart to do
Him homage; speak to Him about your spiritual life,
gazing upon Him in your soul where He is present for
your happiness; welcome Him as warmly as possible, and
behave outwardly in such a way that your actions may give
proof to all of His Presence." (St. Francis de Sales)*[10]

[10] Posted at AZ Quotes, accessed July 31, 2020, https://www.azquotes.com/quote/1056173?ref=holy-eucharist.

When I was about to make my First Holy Communion, my Catholic school offered the opportunity to purchase religious items to mark the occasion. They turned one of our larger classrooms into a mini religious-goods store filled with all sorts of items, including white gloves, white Rosaries, Holy Communion remembrance books, and religious jewelry, along with small statues of the saints, the Blessed Mother, and Jesus.

I can remember walking into the room and my mother's encouragement to buy something that I really wanted, something special that would help me recall this significant moment of my life. I think we were both surprised by my choice. I have always been a girly girl who loves her share of bling. But I didn't make a dash toward the delicate bracelets or lace gloves. Instead, it was a statue that caught my eye and tugged at my heart. It was Jesus holding a chalice. At the bottom of the statue were two adorable angels and below them the words "Panis Angelicus" – Latin for "the bread of angels."

Decades later, I still have that statue and was thinking about it not too long ago during Mass. My husband and I are blessed to be back in our home parish, the same one where I went to school. As I was looking up at the altar and the image of the resurrected Christ, the same image I saw walking up the aisle to receive Jesus in the Eucharist for the first time, an upcoming talk that I would be giving in the spring also came to mind. While I have never mentioned my statue during my reversion story, in reflecting on the journey of this statue and its impact on my life and faith, I just felt I had to work it into my presentation somehow. After all, even though it's now in two pieces, the main part of the statue is still under my pillow. That's the same place it has been since I walked into that makeshift store and insisted that I had to have it. It traveled with me to college, our first apartment, our first home, and our current home, where my husband and I have lived now for twenty-six years. Despite falling away from the Church for some time, I still received comfort and encouragement knowing the statue was there. And once I came back home to my religious roots, I realized the statue was a reminder that Jesus was and is always with me, no matter what.

It was a miracle of sorts that I never lost that statue despite all the packing, unpacking, cleaning, and the regular day-to-day activities of a busy household that cause many treasured items to disappear every now and then. And this was what I was pondering and pray-ing about during Mass: how to incorporate this little miracle into my presentation. I wanted to express how God can use all sorts of items, images, and experiences to let us know that He means what He says. It was then that suddenly I noticed the hymn that was being sung. It's not one that we hear very often anymore at Mass, and if we do hear it, it's usually during the holidays or at weddings (and this was during Ordinary Time). The hymn was none other than "Panis Angelicus." It was written in the thirteenth century by St. Thomas Aquinas in honor of the feast of Corpus Christi, which is connected to the Eucharistic miracle in Orvieto, Italy.

It was hard for me to maintain my composure. What are the chances that beautiful hymn (again, one not heard very often) would be sung right as I was thinking about my Panis Angelicus statue? Oh, and did I mention that this was just days before I headed back to Italy to lead a pilgrimage, with my first stop being none other than the beautiful Etruscan town of Orvieto? It was no coincidence but another Godcidence or "God-wink." It was indeed a hug from heaven and an early Christmas present, one that I will never forget.

REFLECTIONS

———

FROM SCRIPTURE

*"Therefore, since we are receiving
a kingdom that cannot be shaken,
let us be thankful, and so worship
God acceptably with reverence and
awe." (Hebrews 12:28, NIV)*

———

QUESTIONS

When was the last time you
expressed gratitude to God?

What are you most grateful
for in your life right now?

What are some ways you can express
that gratitude to God more regularly?

Are you aware that expressing
gratitude is a form of prayer?

As the saying goes, do you see your
glass as half-empty or half-full? Why?

How is your prayer life?

Have you ever heard from God when you
didn't think you were actually praying?

Do you spend some time in prayer
before and during Mass?

From Financial Fear to Trust in God

BY GAIL BUCKLEY BARRINGER ("THE BIBLE LADY")

WORDS OF WISDOM

God never abandons us, and worrying is not only a waste of time; it's an affront to Our Lord.

SAINTLY ADVICE

"God commands you to pray, but forbids you to worry." (St. Francis de Sales)

GAIL BUCKLEY BARRINGER is the founder and president of Catholic Scripture Study International. For seven years, Gail was president of the Catholic Leadership Coalition and served on the board of Catholics United for the Faith. Gail hosted *The Bible Lady* show on Radio Maria and for the last eight years has been doing the "Scripture Verse of the Week" segment on Ave Maria Radio/EWTN's *Catholic Connection* with Teresa Tomeo. Gail is a member of the Catholic Speakers Bureau and has spoken at several national Catholic conferences. She has also been a featured guest on Catholic radio shows including *Catholic Answers Live*, Ave Maria Radio/EWTN's *Kresta in the Afternoon*, and EWTN's *Deep in Scripture* with Marcus Grodi, and she has appeared on Sacred Heart Radio, Relevant Radio, and Carolina Catholic Radio. Television shows that have featured Gail include the EWTN programs *The Journey Home* with Marcus Grodi, *EWTN Live* with Fr. Mitch Pacwa, *EWTN Bookmark* with Doug Keck, and *The Catholic View for Women*. She's been profiled in the *National Catholic Register* and *Lay Witness* and *Envoy* magazines. In May 2009, Gail was invited to the Vatican for a private audience with Pope Benedict XVI. In 2010, Gail was inducted into the Equestrian Order of the Knights and Ladies of the Holy Sepulchre, an ancient order under the papacy. Learn more about Gail and the Catholic Scripture Study program at www.cssprogram.net and https://www.saintbenedictpress.com/catholic-scripture-study-international.html.

My late husband, Tom, was a very popular and well-respected veterinarian. He had a one-man practice, so whenever he was ill, he would hire another veterinarian to fill in for him at his animal hospital. Unfortunately, he had a bad heart, and over the years, he was hospitalized several times. Whenever this happened, most of his clients would wait until he was back at work to bring in their pets, not because they didn't trust the vet who was filling in, but because they loved Tom so much and preferred to wait. While we appreciated their loyalty, this hurt us financially, since we still had to pay the substitute veterinarian, the staff, and, of course, the office costs—rent, electricity, and so on.

One day, while Tom was treating a cat, it bit his hand. This wasn't the first time he'd been bitten, so as before, he put antibiotic cream on the wound and assumed it would heal. It didn't; it got much worse. He was hospitalized, and an infectious-disease specialist was called. Tom had something much worse than cat-scratch fever, but the doctors were never able to determine just what it was. As the infection spread, I was told more than once that Tom's arm might have to be removed.

Tom's mind was also affected. He didn't know who or where he was. He developed congestive heart failure and kidney failure and was put on dialysis. I was told he might die. Miraculously, nine weeks and eleven surgeries later, he was released from the hospital but remained under home treatment; a nurse came in three times a week. He regained his memory but still seemed somewhat confused.

Unfortunately, during Tom's hospitalization, many clients were waiting for his return to bring in their pets. Others, because he was hospitalized so long, ended up going somewhere else, thinking he was never going to return. During this time, Tom was not receiving any income. Every month, his office manager would alert me that there wasn't enough money in the clinic's bank account to pay the bills, so I would withdraw money from our personal account to cover the balance.

Thanks be to God, after four months, Tom was well enough to return to work. Sadly, his business was hurting financially, but he loved his work and convinced me that he just needed a little time to turn things around.

Before long, however, the office manager started calling me with concerns about how Tom was running the business. She said he was ordering things that they didn't need or couldn't afford and that he was asking clients the same question two or three times. He seemed confused. I realized he had been doing some strange things at home as well, so I convinced him to see a doctor. The doctor sent us to a neurologist, and after several tests, we were given the devastating news that Tom had Alzheimer's disease. We both broke down and cried. On the way home, Tom told me that eventually, I would need to put him in a nursing home. I said I would never do that. He insisted that he wouldn't know anyway and that he didn't want me to have to care for him. I told him, "No, I'll never put you in a nursing home."

There was no way Tom could continue to work, so we needed to close the animal hospital. We were renting the building, and our lease was coming up for renewal soon, so I called the rental agent. He said that we needed to renew the lease for five years as we'd been doing. I explained to him that Tom had been diagnosed with Alzheimer's disease and couldn't possibly continue to practice, so there was no way we could renew our lease. He said he was sorry, but there was nothing he could do: we'd need to evacuate the building within two weeks.

Two weeks?! The practice and equipment were worth several hundred thousand dollars. Two weeks wasn't enough time to advertise the practice for sale, much less sell any of the expensive equipment! Consequently, Tom had to walk away from forty years of work with absolutely nothing, except his reputation as a great veterinarian.

I didn't know how we were going to make ends meet, since my apostolate, Catholic Scripture Study International, was also suffering financially. I had to take over paying the bills. It was then that I realized that not only had Tom not brought home any pay for well over a year, but we were almost $300,000 in debt from the animal hospital bills. How were we ever going to be able to dig out of this hole? My son made a few phone calls and was able to get some of the debt owed to pharmaceutical companies and others reduced or remediated, but I wasn't able to sustain my business and take a salary for myself, so we had no income.

I prayed and prayed and finally resigned myself to the inevitable. We were going to be homeless. I couldn't see any way out. I prayed: "Lord, I don't want to be homeless, but as you know, there's no way I can pay off our debts. We've been blessed and are very thankful, and if this is your will for us now, so be it." Even though I should have been afraid and worried, I felt at peace. And it helped that one of my favorite Scripture passages is Matthew 6:25–34, in which Our Lord tells us not to worry and to have faith that God will take care of us. And all throughout Scripture, God tells us, "Fear not!" Pope St. John Paul II frequently reminds us of this.

The day after my prayer, I received an e-mail from a friend who was the vice president (now president) of a very large Catholic publishing company. He wanted to discuss a business proposition. To my knowledge, he was unaware of my husband's illness, and he definitely couldn't have known about our financial situation, as I hadn't told anyone yet. We met and made an agreement whereby I would still own Catholic Scripture Study International, but his company would take over running CSS and pay me a generous salary for the next two years. After two years, I would receive royalties for the rest of my life. This not only gave me a stable income but allowed me to care for my husband full-time. Sadly, Tom passed away a couple of years later, but I kept my promise to him: I cared for him until the day he died and never put him in a nursing home.

God is always with us, just as He was with the Israelites in the desert. I, too, was in the wilderness, but He was with me. I hope my story will strengthen the faith of others. Do not be afraid: God is with you always.

REFLECTIONS

———

FROM SCRIPTURE

*"Rejoice in hope, endure
in affliction, persevere in
prayer." (Romans 12:12, NABRE)*

"Trust in the Lord *with all your
heart and do not lean on your
own understanding. In all your
ways acknowledge him, and he
will make straight your paths."
(Proverbs 3:5–6, ESV)*

*"Do not fear, for I am with you;
do not be dismayed, for I am your
God. I will strengthen you and
help you." (Isaiah 41:10, NIV)*

QUESTIONS

In Matthew 6:34, Jesus taught: "Therefore do not be anxious about tomorrow, for tomorrow will be anxious for itself. Let the day's own trouble be sufficient for the day." He goes on to tell us never to worry. In what ways does your worrying about the future hamper your ability to be responsive to the present? What steps can you take to rid your life of anxiety and to focus more intently on each moment?

Jesus was tempted just as we are, and the night before His arrest, He prayed to God the Father to take "this cup of passion" from Him. However, He ended His prayer with the words "Not my will, but yours, be done" (Luke 22:42). Like all of us, Jesus did not desire suffering, but He knew God's will was for the best. Can you accept God's will when you pray, knowing that it is always for our greatest good, even if we can't understand it?

Philippians 4:6 tells us not to be anxious about anything, but, with prayer and thanksgiving, to make our requests known to God. This goes for our financial problems as well. God may not answer your prayers for financial provision the way you'd like or as soon as you'd like, but remember, He is always with you. How can you make an effort to notice the signs that God is present in your life? Can you make time to reflect on all the good things He has done for you? Is it difficult for you to trust that He will provide, and if so, why?

Remember when Jesus called St. Peter to come to Him on the water? When St. Peter took his eyes off Jesus and started worrying about the wind and the waves, he began to sink. Immediately, Jesus caught him and asked, "O you of little faith, why did you doubt?" (Matt. 14:31). Have you acted like this when you pray? Do you take your eyes off Him, start worrying, and lose faith that Jesus will answer? In Matthew 17:20, Jesus said if you have faith the size of a grain of mustard seed, nothing will be impossible for you. Reflect on how much you can grow your faith by trusting Jesus and not worrying.

9

Six Years: Thank You for Bringing Me Home

BY ALYSSA BORMES

WORDS OF WISDOM

Our God is a God of infinite wisdom. He gave me a series of single choices, which built one upon the other.

SAINTLY ADVICE

"Do not be afraid. Open wide the doors for Christ....
Do not be afraid. Christ knows 'what is in man.'
He alone knows it." (Pope John Paul II)[11]

---

[11] Homily of His Holiness John Paul II for the Inauguration of His Pontificate, October 22, 1978.

ALYSSA BORMES is an educator, author, speaker, radio host, and retreat leader. She teaches theology at Chesterton Academy in Hopkins, Minnesota; writes for the WINE: Women in the New Evangelization blog; hosts the weekly show *Catholic Kaleidoscope* on Radio Maria; and is the author of *The Catechism of Hockey*. You can find her at AlyssaBormes.com.

It was May 2005. I received an e-mail from a friend who was worried about her husband and his disengagement in their marriage. In an attempt to comfort her, I told her something I once heard: great days and terrible days are connected. By way of example, I intended to tell her of a great day and a terrible day that connected two eras of my life.

It was 2004, and I had been living and going to school in Rome for about a month. A call came to our residence inviting us to meet Pope John Paul II. Later that evening, we were in the Holy Father's library. Having caught my first glimpse of him, I realized how much he was suffering. He would die five months later. When I met him, I knelt before him and said, "Thank you for bringing me home."

I had only recently recovered from the dark years of my life. There were perhaps twenty-five such years, seventeen of which were utterly black. Yet there I was before His Holiness, thanking him. Not only had he been an inspiration to me, but he had inspired so many priests who helped me come home. And he had made my spiritual father, Bishop Paul Dudley, a bishop. Yes—thank you for bringing me home!

Then, I told my friend about an awful day in 1998. I was lying in the fetal position on the shower floor; the hot water was long gone. Perhaps, I hoped, I would die if I stayed there long enough.

Then, there was an urging—not a voice, just an urging—to shut off the water. I obeyed but remained on the floor, waiting for death. A bit later, there was another urging to stand up, dry off, and go to bed. This time, I felt as if a gentle hand were guiding me. It was only late morning, but I slept.

Later that evening, there was a Halloween party at my house. It was terrible to get through, but I was still alive at the end of the day, which at the time felt a bit like both a victory and a defeat. My desire for death was still there, but it wasn't presently boiling over.

As I recounted this story, my heart stopped for a second. Halloween. The terrible party had been on October 31, 1998. I met the pope on October 31, 2004. I realized the simple lesson. With God, I was on a need-to-know basis. On that awful day in 1998, all He did was urge me to shut off the water, dry off, put on my pajamas, and sleep—steps that seemed so small but were actually enormous given the darkness I was in. God did not tell me I would kiss the ring of the pope. If He had, I think I would have desired all the more to die. So much in my life would have to change just to bring me to a place where an invitation to meet the pope was possible. Our God is a God of infinite wisdom. He gave me a series of single choices, which built one upon the other.

Over time, the same happened for my friend and her husband. A series of choices allowed their marriage to heal. In my 2005 e-mail to her, I saw that I had come from not only an era of darkness into one of light, but from a *day* of darkness into another day of light. There was absolutely nothing in me on that day I lay on the shower floor that believed I would ever be worthy to meet the pope. But God knew. All I did was follow Him step by step. I physically and spiritually left that shower floor of despair, and six years to the day later (nearly to the hour, considering the time change), I kissed the ring of the pope. Oh, yes—thank you for bringing me home!

REFLECTIONS

FROM SCRIPTURE

"Though I walk in the midst of dangers,
you guard my life when my enemies rage.
You stretch out your hand;
your right hand saves me.
The LORD is with me to the end.
LORD, your mercy endures forever.
Never forsake the work of your
hands!" (Psalm 138:7–8, NABRE)

QUESTIONS

What simple steps do you think God
is asking you to take right now in
order to deepen your relationship
with Him and His Church?

Do you see your life with God as a
continual journey of growth, or are you
concentrating too much on the future?

God told Alyssa to get up and go to
bed, just as He told the prophets of old
to go and eat, or gather wood—again,
the simple necessities of life. How do
you see God working in the everyday,
practical matters of your life in order
to keep you moving forward?

How are you learning to enjoy the
journey more than you have in the past?

The Accident That Was No Accident

BY JULIE PEROLIO

WORDS OF WISDOM

*Do what God asks you to do. We may not always see His
results, but we've still planted the seed He has asked us
to plant. His plan is greater than our own knowledge. I
was blessed to learn that lesson early in counseling. Get
over yourself and let God work! And pray, pray, pray!*

SAINTLY ADVICE

*"Pray, hope, and don't worry. Worry is useless. God is
merciful and will hear your prayers." (St. Padre Pio)*

JULIE PEROLIO was born and raised in Port Huron, Michigan. She moved to the Detroit area in 1973 and converted to Catholicism in 1985. She has two wonderful sons and a beautiful daughter, five terrific stepchildren, and eight perfect grandchildren. In 1996, Julie became a volunteer and peer counselor at Pregnancy Aid in Detroit, where she volunteered for twelve years, six of them as president. Julie also taught abstinence and chastity in many local schools and youth groups. In 2004, Julie lost her beloved husband, Pete Hage, to cancer. Julie remarried in 2008, and now resides in Fort Wayne, Indiana, with her wonderful husband, Steve Perolio, and continues to advocate for the unborn. Julie is vice-president of the board of Right to Life of Northeast Indiana (www.ichooselife.org).

It was my first day as a peer counselor. Today, I was supposed to shadow someone with experience. She got sick and didn't show.

As always, we prayed before opening the clinic, and as soon as the doors opened, we had several young ladies waiting.

My first-ever client needed a pregnancy test. Easy. I could do that. It was positive, but she already knew that and was scheduled for an abortion the next day. She said that no matter what, she was having that abortion. I asked her what brought her in that morning, given that she had already made up her mind. She said she was driving by, saw our sign, and just decided to stop. I tried to talk her into an ultrasound. At the time, we had a doctor on Eight Mile Road who would do it for free. I begged her, to no avail.

Before she left, I told her that she would need to talk to someone the next day: she would be feeling sad and depressed. I gave her my cellphone number, and then I asked her if I could pray with her. She agreed.

I sat in the office crying after she left. I didn't say enough. I wasn't good enough. Maybe I wasn't cut out to do this. I couldn't convince her to go get the ultrasound. (Me, me, me!)

The next day, she called me at about noon. I was expecting crying and despair but instead heard joy. That's when she told me she was driving her boyfriend to work that morning, when someone ran a red light on Gratiot Avenue, a major road that runs through the metro Detroit area, and plowed into the side of their car. The police arrived, and the first thing they asked was, "Are you pregnant?"

Without even considering what she planned to do in a couple of hours, she answered yes. An ambulance came and rushed her to the hospital for an emergency ultrasound—something I couldn't talk her into. She saw her baby formed and perfect. She completely believed that her baby waved at her. In tears of joy, she said, "We are keeping our baby!"

What did I learn? Just because I was done with her didn't mean God was! Get over yourself, Julie! It wasn't about me! Love people where they are. Do what the Lord asks of you. Pray and get out of His way!

REFLECTIONS

FROM SCRIPTURE

"Trust in the Lord with all your heart, and do not lean on your own understanding." (Proverbs 3:5, ESV)

QUESTIONS

Are you obedient to God's plan, even when it looks impossible?

Do you share God's blessings as a light to others?

Do you follow up on difficult situations? Or do you give up … just because you think you've failed?

His Grace Is Sufficient

BY FR. ANDREW DAWSON

WORDS OF WISDOM

I recall sitting in the confessional one day, listening to a defeated-sounding penitent, and hearing God tell me very clearly that this man and this moment were the reason I had struggled through seminary. As I counseled the penitent and assured him of God's love for him, I thanked the Lord for my six years of study and discernment, the struggles I had experienced, and this revelation of how He intended to use my suffering and my weaknesses for His glory.

SAINTLY ADVICE

"He who trusts himself is lost. He who trusts God can do all things." (St. Alphonsus Liguori)

FR. ANDREW DAWSON, originally from Yorkshire, England, has lived in Michigan for the past twenty-five years. Born into a Baptist family (although his father is now a retired Anglican priest), he is the second of three children. In 2006, Fr. Dawson joined the Catholic Church, making him the only Catholic in his family. The Real Presence of Jesus in the Eucharist was his biggest "Protestant struggle" with the Catholic Faith as well as the foundation of his conversion. He entered Sacred Heart Major Seminary in 2011 and was ordained a priest in six years later. His favorite saints are St. Peter, St. John Vianney, and St. Ignatius of Loyola, each of whom significantly helped him discern his vocation. A farmer at heart, Fr. Dawson is gradually restoring a 1946 Farmall tractor. He enjoys working with his hands, building, drawing, singing, watching auto-racing, and fishing.

When was the last time you thanked God for your failure? When did you last celebrate a weakness?

A number of years ago, an article entitled "Are you weak enough to be a priest?" was making the rounds in the seminary. Its premise was that we've secularized our lives into a soup of talents and desires and opportunities. We live in a society that judges and values someone's abilities as qualifications for a career or path through life. But it's detrimental for a person discerning a religious vocation to ignore his weaknesses.

The author of the article, Fr. Michael Buckley, S.J., who died last year, writes:

> Weakness more profoundly relates us to God, because it provides the ambit or the arena in which his grace can be seen, in which his sustaining presence can reveal itself, in which even his power can become manifest.... Weakness is the context for the epiphany of the Lord ... not always as felt reassurance, but more often as a power to continue, faithful even when we do not feel the strength.... Jesus Christ is enough.

My three years as a priest have shown me how spot-on that article was.

It's often only because of our weaknesses and inabilities that we come to see ourselves in the light of truth. We are people in need of God's grace, and we hold all the cards: we can either shut Him out or let Him in and allow Him to fulfill in us whatever we lack.

Discipleship, conversion of life, is never a sleigh ride. It takes spiritual stamina and endurance. It's work. It's not easy. At the heart of it is struggle. So how do we endure? How do we find the stamina to pick ourselves up and keep struggling?

The Israelites were probably asking themselves this question in their days of exile in Babylon. Through the prophet Isaiah, God gave His answer. He invited His people back to Jerusalem. But their homes and everything from their old lives lay in ruins, and they were reluctant to return from exile. Even though Jerusalem was home, to return would require too much work and pain and difficulty.

In response, Isaiah speaks of the abundant resources God wants to give His people out of His mercy:

> All you who are thirsty, come to the water! You who have no money, come, buy grain and eat; come, buy grain without money, wine and milk without cost! Why spend your money for what is not bread; your wages for what does not satisfy? Only listen to me, and you shall eat well; you shall delight in rich fare. Pay attention and come to me; listen, that you may have life. I will make with you an everlasting covenant, the steadfast loyalty promised to David. (55:1-3, NABRE)

All you who are thirsty, who have no money, come, and *I* will feed you. This is poetic and metaphorical language. God will bless His people abundantly not only with basic physical necessities but with Himself, the only One who can satisfy when all their own efforts, their spent wages, have failed. God is encouraging them: "Come to me, and let me save you. Watch while I provide for you."

In the Gospel, Jesus teaches His disciples a similar lesson when He feeds thousands of people with five loaves and two fish (echoing the Last Supper and the Eucharist, which we celebrate every Sunday). I'm sure the disciples wanted to know how they could possibly feed so many with so little. It's a reasonable concern. We can imagine their protest: "We're not miracle-workers here, Jesus!" But we can also imagine His response: "No, you're not. But I'm setting you up to be, and for that, you need to know that you need me!"

Jesus wants His disciples to come to grips with their own insufficiency. He wants them to realize, too, that through Him, they can do all things. Or, more accurately, through us, God can do all things. The grace of Our Lord Jesus Christ makes possible that which is impossible for us on our own. But it takes a conscious acceptance of His invitation: "Let me in. Let me work through you. Let me surprise you." And where does that grace come from? From the Eucharist, from the sacraments—God's free gift of Himself to the thirsty, to the hungry, to all of us who know we can't do it by ourselves.

I had been a priest only two months, and in my first parish only one month, when I had experienced a series of events that rocked me. I didn't expect these things to happen until twenty years into my priesthood, but in succession, over a two-week period, there they all were, and I had to call on all the skills I had. And I knew I was coming up short. I knew that everything I had was not enough. Seminary had not prepared me for this.

One of these incidents happened one Sunday afternoon. I wasn't the celebrant for the noon Mass, so I decided to go to the choir room and check on the children's Breaking Open the Word session. The room was empty; I had the schedule wrong.

But that mistake, coupled with my decision to stay for a bit to play the piano and then leave through a door I didn't generally use, meant I crossed paths with a man I had not seen before. I'll call him Jim. Jim was staggering across the parking lot midway through Mass, clutching his chest, his face contorted in pain.

To make a long story short, Jim was under severe stress. His wife had left him, taking with her his life savings, which was a considerable sum of money. Last night, he'd come close to taking his own life. But for some reason, he decided to come to Mass.

When a phone vibrated during the liturgy, Jim thought it was his. Maybe his wife was calling. When he found out the phone belonged to someone else, that was the final straw.

And now I found myself alone, out of sight behind a wall, with a man in tears, pleading with me to let him go so he could end his life.

I have never been more aware of my insufficiency and my need for the Holy Spirit to tell me what to say. When I need my words, they usually don't come. I'm Winnie the Pooh with the honey pot stuck on my head, saying, "Lord, I got nothing!" But in that moment, I knew the things I was saying had to come from someone else.

I told Jim only five things, over and over. Essentially, I said, "You have value, your life is important, God loves you, I love you, and things *will* get better." At the end of our conversation, Jim said I'd told him more about God in forty-five minutes than he'd heard in seventy years.

I was also sneaky enough to get his license plate before he left (trust, but verify)! I talked to him by phone several more times that day, and praise God, had lunch with him the next day. Later, I saw him at Mass again—with his wife.

None of that was due to my counseling skills, which were found wanting. God was the counselor, and I was calling out in faith for His help. And I received it in abundance. I just took the little I had—my five loaves and two fish, my presence, my willingness to listen—and handed it over to God to let Him make something of it. And the Lord made something beautiful to satisfy that desperate man.

The growth of God's life in us through the Eucharist does not usually happen overnight. God's grace seeps in slowly, almost unnoticed. Only later, when we go through some challenge or crisis or tragedy, do we realize the astonishing spiritual strength we received from the Lord. This shouldn't be a surprise. St. Paul's powerful prayer in his Letter to the Romans confirms that God's power has always been available to us: "In all these things we conquer overwhelmingly through him who loved us. For I am convinced that neither death, nor life, nor angels, nor principalities, nor present things, nor future things, nor powers, nor height, nor depth, nor any other creature will be able to separate us from the love of God in Christ Jesus our Lord" (8:37–39, NABRE).

In a time when the world's resources are supposedly being over-consumed, we should tap into the most underused resource of heaven: the grace of God. It's powerful, it's free, and it's available in abundance.

REFLECTIONS

FROM SCRIPTURE

*"But we hold this treasure in earthen
vessels, that the surpassing power
may be of God and not from us."*
(2 Corinthians 4:7, NABRE)

QUESTIONS

Do you have too narrow a view of the
gifts God has given you or someone else?

Are you rejecting as a weakness
a quality that God has bestowed
on you and through which He
intends to work for His glory?

What is your first response to realizing
you are "in over your head"? Do you
think of your own insufficiencies,
or do you reach out for the grace
of the Holy Spirit bestowed on you
at Baptism and Confirmation?

Have you noticed God's presence when
you least expected and most needed
Him? Have you thanked Him?

Do you overcomplicate the Faith?
What are five simple things you could
be ready now to tell someone who
needs to know that God loves him?

In the Shadow of the Cross

BY VANESSA DENHA GARMO

WORDS OF WISDOM

*God is everywhere, and once you put your faith
in Him, He will always have your back.*

SAINTLY ADVICE

*"Right is right even if no one is doing it; wrong is
wrong even if everyone is doing it."* (St. Augustine)

VANESSA DENHA GARMO is a communications strategist, evangelist, coach, content creator, and storyteller. She is the founder of Epiphany Communications & Coaching and the Communications Evangelist Institute, where she serves as a communications and public relations consultant, coach, and media trainer. She earned a master's degree in communications and coaches clients on careers, leadership, communications, and reaching goals. She hosts workshops on how to get an interview and how to be interviewed, public speaking, and networking, as well as leadership and communication strategies. She has an extensive background in both print and broadcast news as well as video production, and produces television programs for various media outlets around the globe. She is an award-winning journalist, author, and professional speaker. Her extensive media background includes working at WJR 760 AM as a general street reporter, news anchor, and health reporter. She created and hosted the weekly show *Secrets to Good Health* and continues to serve as producer and host of the weekly public service announcement show *It's Your Community* on 96.3 WDVD, 93.1 NASH-FM, and News/Talk 760 WJR. She co-founded the *Chaldean News* and was its co-publisher and editor-in-chief for nearly sixteen years. As press secretary and main spokesperson to the Wayne County Executive Office, Vanessa handled media relations, speech writing, and crisis communications as well as long-term and short-term public relations and marketing strategies. She is also a voice talent, and her Christ-Centered Communications Messages can be heard daily on Ave Maria Catholic Radio 990 AM. She is a member of the Public Relations Society of America. As a speaker, Vanessa hosts workshops and speaks about the media, social media, networking, and public speaking. Learn more at www.epiphanyccc.com and www.communicationevangelist.com.

I have had one foot in the secular world and one in the Catholic world since 2003. It was the year I left my job as the press secretary to the largest county in Michigan to launch my own communications and coaching company, Epiphany Communications & Coaching. I am a communications strategist, content creator, storyteller, and coach.

It was a true moment of surrender. I carried my family's benefits and was helping my husband build his heating and cooling business. Our daughter was two and a half years old at the time, and when she walked up to me with a box of tissues because I had been crying over the darkness in government, I knew I had to get out. I let go and let God take over.

I often work with media to pitch my clients' stories. I often walk a fine line with the media because of my conservative views. I am a guest host for Teresa Tomeo on Ave Maria Radio, where I also host my own Christ-Centered Communication Messages that air daily. On Teresa's show, I have a regular segment called "In the News" where we discuss current events and media stories from a Catholic perspective and show the bias in some reporting. We also highlight those reporters who are delivering balanced stories. Having one foot in and foot out is not a fun Hokey Pokey dance.

Over the years, I have been challenged on social media by friends on the left, including those working in the media, for making more-conservative posts or just sharing news stories that are not in line with their perspectives. I never experienced more divisiveness and hate than during the COVID-19 crisis. The political divide and mutual disdain were almost palpable.

I am not a Democrat or a Republican. I am conservative on social issues. I am pro-life. I vote for who I think will be the best leader, and I vote with my Christian conscience.

After I posted a news clip from an ABC affiliate in California about two doctors challenging the reports of Dr. Anthony Fauci, a thread of comments was made, some quite condescending. It was the second report on that topic I posted that angered some people, including members of the media, and prompted them to make comments. I appreciate people's perspectives, but attacks against people who don't agree with you are alarming. I've seen posts referring to conservative voters as "hillbillies" receive no claims of offensiveness or inappropriateness, just laughing emojis and heaps of likes. Meanwhile, reporters and freelance journalists continue to post vicious comments. Some seem to issue daily attacks on the president. One freelance writer even posted a photoshopped picture of protesters in Lansing, Michigan, who were protesting the governor's overreaching stay-at-home orders. In the original photo, the men were carrying guns. However, in the picture the writer posted, the guns were replaced with obscene objects. I was appalled and couldn't believe that something like that would be considered acceptable, let alone funny. I thought, "If a conservative posted something like that to ridicule a liberal, wouldn't it spark outrage?"

I know there are conservatives who respond to these attacks with disparaging remarks about liberals. That is not acceptable either. We have lost our civility and decorum in this country. I get challenged for posting legitimate news stories that oppose the Left's view of the pandemic and challenge liberal leaders. Apparently, that is crossing the line, but there's no problem with post after post, including those from members of the media, attacking, insulting, and ridiculing the president.

I can't imagine my bosses tolerating that kind of public behavior when I was working in the secular media. Today, the same reporters who are supposed to be objective and unbiased are using their social media platforms to attack openly the same public figures they are supposed to be covering objectively. "Idiot" and "moron" are common epithets. Yet if I, in a very respectful way, question the authority of Michigan's governor or her decision to keep abortion clinics but not landscaping companies open during the pandemic, I am this horrible person. How dare I challenge her?

One Sunday night, I was emotionally drained.

I was near tears of complete frustration with the social media banter, unfairness, and condescending comments for anyone with a conservative view. I called Teresa Tomeo to vent. Sitting on my oversized brown beanbag, I spent about an hour on the phone discussing the constant attempts to silence opposing voices.

As always, I prayed before bed, and I prayed that next morning, but more intently than usual. My prayer included some venting to God. The last thing I said was: "God, I will do my part, but I am leaving crazy in your hands. I can't deal with crazy anymore."

I got out of bed and started walking to the kitchen to get a cup of coffee. As I walked by my office, I saw in my window a shadow of a large cross that I had never seen before. I immediately felt Jesus patting me on the back and saying: "I got this. I am here. Don't worry."

I can't even write this story without crying. I e-mailed Teresa the photo, and she replied: "V, God is giving you a big hug and intentionally left the message for you in your office where you communicate. Take His sign to heart. He has your back."

I prayed that morning, thanking God for giving me this shadow of a cross as a sign. I felt Him put on my heart the idea to use my social media platforms to evangelize, to talk about Him and to get away from the divisiveness of politics during this crisis. I posted the picture of the cross on my Facebook page with this comment: "Said morning prayers and started walking by my office to get coffee from the kitchen and I get a glimpse of this shadow in the window. A comforting sign in these chaotic times." In a short time, I had nearly 230 likes and a slew of positive comments.

It was my God-wink not of the day but of a lifetime. It will forever be a reminder that He is with me always. I follow Him, and He will have my back. Someone once said that "those who leave things in God's hands will eventually see God's hands in everything." That is my plan!

REFLECTIONS

———

FROM SCRIPTURE

"Have no anxiety at all, but in everything, by prayer and petition, with thanksgiving, make your requests known to God. Then the peace of God that surpasses all understanding will guard your hearts and minds in Christ Jesus." (Philippians 4:6–7, NABRE)

———

QUESTIONS

Look around. Where do you see God's hand in your life?

What moment in your life has been a true occasion of surrender to God?

How can you communicate the truth on social media in a loving, Christ-centered way?

In moments of frustration, do you stop and ask what Jesus would say?

13

You've Got Mail

BY TERESA TOMEO

WORDS OF WISDOM

Scripture and Church teaching affirm the intercession of the saints. Let us not forget to call on them and ask for their prayers and support. You might be pleasantly surprised at how fast and powerfully they respond.

SAINTLY ADVICE

"Praying for others is a sign of love; and the more love the saints in heaven have, the more they pray for those on earth who can be helped by their prayers. And the closer they are to God, the more effective their prayers are." (St. Thomas Aquinas)

Growing up Catholic, I was always surrounded by beautiful images of the saints. While I admired those statues and pictures, I didn't begin to take the intercession of the saints seriously until much later in life. Eventually, after studying Church teaching, reading biographies, and having the opportunity to visit the birthplaces of many of our great saints on pilgrimage, I've grown in my relationship with them, and I consider them heavenly friends who accompany me on my earthly journey. I've had so many wonderful experiences with the saints, especially my all-time favorite, St. Teresa of Avila, after whom I was named. One story stands out among the rest: the timing was so perfect and the response to my call for help so swift, it took my breath away and still does whenever I think about or share the story.

As you may recall, several years ago, the Religious Freedom Restoration Act (RFRA) was being debated and revisited in states such as Indiana and my home state of Michigan. All the way back in 1993, Congress passed the RFRA with bipartisan support to protect religious freedom. Some feared the measure was being used to discriminate against certain groups of people, including those with same-sex attraction. As a Catholic talk-show host, I'm frequently called up to take part in secular media interviews on faith-based topics. This time, I was asked to be interviewed for a news story about the RFRA that would include the reaction of the local Christian community. Even with decades of news experience under my belt, I find it challenging to be on the other side of the camera or microphone, as you never know what is going to end up on air. In this case, I knew the reporter and figured if anyone would give me a fair shake, it would be him.

I wasn't asking for any favors; I just hoped he would do his job in accurately reflecting both sides of a very sensitive story.

My hopes were not only dashed; they were tossed onto the newsroom floor and then stomped on. The story that aired on the news that night was nothing short of a total hatchet job, as we say in the business. The reporter and editors did their best to twist my words and portray me as some sort of a religious zealot or hatemonger. I was all the more surprised because, as always, I recorded my interview and even told the reporter that I was doing so. And yet he still decided to present a narrative quite different from reality.

I called the reporter and spoke to him about the blatant way he took my words out of context. He vehemently denied any wrongdoing, but apparently, his viewers disagreed. Unbeknownst to me, as we were speaking, dozens of viewers were calling the TV station to complain—so much so that the next day, I received a call from his producer, apologizing and asking me to come back later in the week to be part of their public affairs show, which was going to dive into the topic even more deeply. The program aired live at ten-thirty eastern on Thursday nights. But that Thursday wasn't just any Thursday. It was Holy Thursday. The producer needed to know by four or five that afternoon at the latest if I would be willing to join them.

My first inclination was to tell the station nicely to go jump in a lake. Why would I subject myself to such biased reporting again, and on Holy Thursday of all days? I honestly didn't know what to do. I realized that doing a live interview would prevent them from chopping and distorting my statements as they had done in the previous interview, but it was still a tough choice. So I called on St. Teresa of Avila.

It was around three in the afternoon—the Hour of Mercy when Jesus died on the Cross. I was a nervous wreck. Part of me felt very guilty. This was Holy Week, after all, and if Our Lord could suffer so greatly for me and the rest of humanity, wasn't I being a wimp in not wanting to march into the studio for another interview? My concerns seemed so trivial compared to the big picture. Then again, I wanted to present an accurate representation of the Catholic Church's view on the RFRA debate.

I walked into our living room, stood in front of a beautiful icon of St. Teresa of Avila, and just poured my heart out with prayers that went something like this: "Okay, St. Teresa. I really need your help, and fast. Please intercede for me and ask the Lord to give me a sign. If He wants me to do this interview, I will. If He wants me to remain silent, that's fine too. Just ask Him as quickly as possible to give me a sign. I'm really stressed as to what I should do."

After saying the prayer, I felt much better. I decided that if I didn't feel any promptings or receive any type of encouragement in the next hour, I needed to walk away from the interview offer. To be honest, I was secretly hoping I could call the station back and say, "Thanks, but no thanks." Instead, I received a very direct answer within ten minutes.

It came in the mail. After praying, I heard the mail being dropped off and went outside on the porch to retrieve it. There was a box with an Easter gift from a dear friend of mine. I was grateful not only for her kindness but for the opportunity to get my mind off the challenge I was facing.

I opened the box to find a bronze plaque of St. Teresa of Avila with the words from her famous prayer, St. Teresa's Bookmark: "Let nothing disturb you. Let nothing frighten you."

I started to laugh and cry at the same time. It was so obvious that it was a direct answer to my prayer. I needed to do the interview and know that God, and St. Teresa, of course, would be with me.

As powerful as the gift was, God and St. Teresa had even more encouragement in store. I had to write my friend and let her know what just transpired. I messaged her on Facebook and explained how her gift was such a timely, wonderful answer to prayer. What she told me next almost knocked me off my chair.

"I can't believe you received the package today," she wrote. "It's only Thursday. I just sent the package late Tuesday. The post office insisted that it most likely wouldn't arrive until Saturday at best, and most likely not until Easter Monday, given the busy time of year. That's amazing."

We serve an amazing God, and we are surrounded by an amazing cloud of witnesses, including more than ten thousand Catholic saints. And there I was, worried about one little interview, which, by the way, went very well.

> Let nothing disturb you,
> Let nothing frighten you,
> All things are passing;
> God only is changeless.
> Patience gains all things.
> Nothing is wanting in him who possesses God.
> God alone suffices.
> Amen!

REFLECTIONS

———

FROM SCRIPTURE

"When he had taken the scroll, the four living creatures and the twenty-four elders fell down before the Lamb, each holding a harp, and with golden bowls full of incense, which are the prayers of the saints." *(Revelation 5:8)*

———

QUESTIONS

If you were to list five of your favorite saints, who would they be and why?

What type of guidance, intervention, or help have you received from a saint?

Besides interceding for us, what role do the saints play in the spiritual lives of Catholics?

Have you thought about making a pilgrimage to one of the many sites dedicated to the saints?

14

Of Lost Keys and Perilous Car Trips

BY HOPE PONSART HANSEN

WORDS OF WISDOM

I hope readers realize, as I am still learning, that we all have preconceived notions of what God is supposed to do, how He is supposed to respond to and communicate with us. I think it is in letting go—letting things unfold and accepting what comes to us through prayer—that we open opportunities for God to speak to us.

SAINTLY ADVICE

"Let nothing disturb you; | let nothing frighten you. | All things are passing; | God only is changeless. | Patience gains all things. | Nothing is wanting to him who possesses God. | God alone suffices." (St. Teresa of Avila)

HOPE PONSART HANSEN spent the majority of her career as a television writer and producer for various network affiliates around the country. After retiring, she freelanced for several years, then led a business revitalization effort as director of the downtown development authority for the town of Holly, Michigan. Promoting a town was one of the most exciting experiences that she has been blessed to have! She also spent time developing special events and sponsorships for Hurley Hospital in Flint, Michigan. She has now found a spiritual and professional home with the Marian Fathers of the Immaculate Conception in Stockbridge, Massachusetts, as a donor relations officer. As a volunteer with Paradise Animal Rescue in Lapeer, Michigan, she takes care of dogs and helps with fundraising and promotion. Hope enjoys spending time with family and friends, volunteer work, gardening, and biking. Hope lives in Davison, Michigan, with her husband John and their grumpy cat Callie. Contact Hope at hopeponsart@gmail.com.

Over a year ago, I began my journey into the Catholic Faith. I am blessed to work for the Marian Fathers of the Immaculate Conception in Stockbridge, Massachusetts. Speaking with faithful people every day and assisting with parish missions made me curious, and I began to learn about Catholicism and Divine Mercy. I credit several folks for motivating me to take, literally, a leap of faith. One is Fr. Chris Alar, a Marian priest who encouraged me to learn about and embrace the Marians and their mission. Another is my friend Teresa Tomeo, who is an amazing example of truly living the Catholic life. Yet another is my husband, John Hansen, a cradle Catholic who is growing with me in the Faith.

I signed up for RCIA classes at St. John the Evangelist in Davison, Michigan. For me, one of the Faith's greatest sources of mystery was our Marian seminarians. These are inspirational, faith-filled young men who answered a call. I always ask them: "What kind of call was it? How did God speak to you? Was it a voice? A gong? A feeling?" They always have a story—a voice, a powerful feeling, an event.

Our benefactors, too, share their stories with me about their experiences of hearing God's voice. Some have even had visions and visitations.

"Why the heck don't I have some kind of clear 'message?' " I wondered.

I wanted a vision, a visit, a loud thump against the wall—*something!* Then, it happened, and it wasn't what I expected.

The first time was while we were learning about various saints in RCIA. The Catholic Church has a *lot* of saints—hundreds of them. I had a hard time believing that all these folks were helping God, the same God who said "you shall have no other gods before me" (Exod. 20:3). Why would He need all this help?

One morning, as I was thinking about this question, I got a call from my ninety-one-year-old mom, with whom I live while working at the office in Stockbridge. It's a beautiful arrangement, as I am able to help her remain in our family home, and my job allows me to take a couple of weeks to be with my husband in Michigan, visit our Midwestern donors, and work in my home office.

Mom told me she couldn't find her car keys (don't worry: she only drives to the post office, the town dump, and a small grocery store). I could tell she was upset. I left work to help her look for the missing keys. After an hour of searching truly *everywhere*, I said in exasperation, "Okay, if there really are saints and they really do help us, I'm calling on St. Anthony, my guardian angel, anyone listening, to please help me find these car keys."

Seriously, no more than five minutes later, I was *compelled* to go out to the garage, locate the blue recycle bin, and turn it upside down. I began sifting through the plastic and cans. Lo and behold, there were the car keys. That was the end of my saints conundrum.

As I continued my studies, I began to pray more, especially the Chaplet of Divine Mercy at three in the afternoon. I love this prayer, and I love saying it with John. I have the Divine Mercy image on the dashboard in my car, and each time I begin the drive between Stockbridge and Michigan, I touch it as a reminder that I can go forward with confidence. At the end of each journey, I thank God for a safe trip and touch the image again.

Recently, a few days before the drive back, my tire-pressure light came on. The last time this happened, the problem turned out to be the sensor in the spare tire. Since I knew I'd be taking the car in for an oil change when I got to Davison, I just made the trip as usual.

The next day, John took my car in for me. I called him in the afternoon to say hi and see if the car needed anything else done. He sounded kind of funny when he said the mechanic did find something, and he'd rather discuss it when he came home. That was weird. I have a very healthy imagination, so by the time John got home, I was pretty sure the car needed new brakes, maybe a new transmission—at the very least, something incredibly expensive.

What he told me took my breath away. He said our mechanic found a large nail in the tire and was amazed that the tire had lasted nine hours on the highway. The mechanic had never seen anything like it: that tire should not have held together. John was amazed and grateful, and he thanked God I made it home safely.

I thought of the story of the footprints in the sand, which reminds us that God is always there, even when we can't see Him. I went outside, looked up at the twilight sky, and whispered, "Jesus, I trust in you." Thinking about it still gives me chills.

My journey is still unfolding. I am so happy to share that on May 31, Pentecost, I made my profession of faith and became a member of the Catholic Church at St. John the Evangelist in Davison, Michigan.

I've learned that God really does speak to us, though maybe not how or when we expect. By letting go of expectations and allowing events to unfold naturally, we will more easily notice God's message.

REFLECTIONS

———

FROM SCRIPTURE

"For God speaks in one way, and in two, though man does not perceive it." (Job 33:14)

"Why do you call me 'Lord, Lord,' and not do what I tell you?" (Luke 6:46)

———

QUESTIONS

Are you really listening to God, or trying to force Him to communicate on your terms?

When God does speak to you, do you resist Him if He doesn't tell you what you want to hear?

Are you sincerely letting go and letting God … or is this just lip service?

What are some ways you can earnestly ask God for help every day, not just when you're in crisis?

Music to God's Ears

BY AL KRESTA

WORDS OF WISDOM

The God who created and governs the cosmos is intimately engaged in the minutest details of our inner lives. Nothing is hidden from His sight. He certainly works dramatically to free us from deadly addictions. But He is equally concerned with our choices in routine situations. He cares whether this particular purchase or entertainment choice will build us up or tear us down. The adventure of discipleship is a daily call to draw closer to Him in the major and minor moments of life.

SAINTLY ADVICE

"It is Jesus in fact that you seek when you dream of happiness; he is waiting for you when nothing else you find satisfies you; he is the beauty to which you are so attracted; it is he who provokes you with that thirst for fullness that will not let you settle for compromise; it is he who urges you to shed the masks of a false life; it is he who reads in your hearts your most genuine choices, the choices that others try to stifle. It is Jesus who stirs in you the desire to do something great with your lives, the will to follow an ideal, the refusal to allow yourselves to be grounded down by mediocrity, the courage to commit yourselves humbly and patiently to improving yourselves and society, making the world more human and more fraternal." (St. John Paul II)[12]

[12] Address of the Holy Father John Paul II at the Vigil of Prayer for the Fifteenth World Youth Day, August 19, 2000, http://w2.vatican.va/content/john-paul-ii/en/speeches/2000/jul-sep/documents/hf_jp-ii_spe_20000819_gmg-veglia.html.

AL KRESTA is a broadcaster, writer, author, and, above all, a missionary. He is president and CEO of Ave Maria Radio and host of *Kresta in the Afternoon*. A 1976 honors graduate of Michigan State University, Al has also done graduate work in theology at both Catholic and Protestant seminaries. He became well known in the Detroit area for his program *Talk from the Heart*, one of the top-rated Christian talk radio programs during the 1980s and 1990s. When he began the program, Al was a Protestant pastor. The questions he was faced with as pastor, however, led him to return to the Catholic Church. His profound personal conversion to Christ and return to the Catholic Church is told in the best-selling anthology *Surprised by Truth*. In 1997, Domino's Pizza founder Tom Monaghan recruited Al to launch the media apostolate Ave Maria Communications.

On *Kresta in the Afternoon*, Al draws upon his distinctive faith background to create what is arguably the most fascinating — and most spiritually constructive — talk show on the radio today. Heard on more than 350 stations and SiriusXM Satellite Radio, *Kresta in the Afternoon* looks at all areas of life through the lens of Scripture and the teaching of the Catholic Church and takes on all comers. Over the years, Al has engaged in vigorous discussions and debates with nationally known figures in politics, the arts, the Church, academia, and business, including Mother Angelica, Jesse Jackson, John McCain, Gloria Steinem, Cuba Gooding Jr., Scott Hahn, Rick Santorum, Judge Robert Bork, Jerry Falwell, Pat Buchanan, Mrs. Anwar Sadat, Martin Luther King III, Jack Kevorkian, John Cardinal O'Connor, Chuck Colson, Archbishop Charles Chaput, George McGovern, C. Everett Koop, Francis Cardinal George, Dennis Quaid, George Will, Tim Russert, Newt

Gingrich, Mike Huckabee, Garrison Keillor, Dion DiMucci, Collin Raye, and many more.

Al's life and spiritual journey took on a new dimension in February 2003, when he lost his left leg to necrotizing fasciitis, an infection often referred to as "flesh-eating disease." His extended recovery and eventual return to broadcasting have given him new insights into the realities of suffering and hope. He is the author of *Dangers to the Faith: Recognizing Catholicism's 21st-Century Opponents; Moments of Grace: Inspiring Stories from Well-Known Catholics; Why Do Catholics Genuflect? And Answers to Other Puzzling Questions About the Catholic Church;* and *Why Are Catholics So Concerned About Sin? More Answers to Puzzling Questions About the Catholic Church.* Al and his wife, Sally, have been married for thirty years and have been blessed with five children on earth and two in heaven. Find Al at AveMariaRadio.net.

W hen seen from the outside, God-moments can appear small and insignificant. But when experienced on the inside, they can be powerful, even life changing. This is one such story, and it requires a long running start.

Sometime in 1964, when I was in eighth grade, I started playing guitar. During the summer between my freshman and sophomore years of high school, I was invited to play lead guitar in a local band — aptly named the Bad Seed — that quickly started performing in dance clubs in Connecticut, Massachusetts, and New York. Most of the band members were already out of high school. I was the youngest, a fairly innocent Catholic kid and anxious to please the older guys. So I was easily influenced. Sex, drugs, and rock 'n' roll went together for my generation the way wine, women, and song did for my parents' generation. And so the Bad Seed bore some bad fruit through my teen years.

In 1969, by God's grace, I made a moral about-face. I knew I had been on the road to destruction. I wanted life, not death. Spiritual things became real for me. I didn't go back to the Catholic Church but tried to find God in more exotic settings. After high school, by age nineteen, I was living a single, celibate, clean, and sober life. I practiced meditation, vegetarianism, and chanting, hoping to ascend to a higher realm of the spirit. At the same time, I began studying jazz guitar and composition at Berklee College of Music in Boston. I dreamed about a future as a musician. But it wasn't to be. My "spiritual" teachers persuaded me that spiritual perfection could be obtained only if I renounced the musical passions of my youth. So

I left Boston and joined what could be called a New Age spiritual community near Battle Creek, Michigan. It was good riddance to my guitar and record collection; they were reduced to grim reminders of the sinister forces that had nearly destroyed me in high school. Obedience to God, as I understood Him at the time, was in direct opposition to my dream of a musical future.

Five years later, in 1974, I had enrolled at Michigan State University. My spiritual search had broadened. I started reading the Bible. In my conversations with fellow students about spiritual and religious things, the Bible kept coming up. Of course it would: the Bible was the most important spiritual document in my own culture, yet I had never studied it. I wanted to change that. But in reading Scripture, I realized, to my dismay, that the Jesus of the New Testament was definitely not the Jesus of the New Age movement. It was time for another turnaround. I became a "Bible-believing" Christian. As I studied God's Word, He began transforming my way of thinking about Him, Christ, celibacy, music, diet, and lots more. The first thing I did was to start worshipping Christ at a nondenominational Bible church. Then, I started enjoying Arby's. Next step was to get myself a new guitar and begin searching for a wife.

In that first year after my conversion to Christ, I came to believe that He was calling me to spend my life disseminating the Christian view of life. At that time, this call was not very specific. I was already sharing my faith in Christ pretty regularly, so maybe I'd be a full-time evangelist. I didn't know. By God's providence, I met Roger and Linda Stieg, a husband and wife team, both violinists who were spiritually hungry. As we talked, they received the gospel, and we formed a trio that strolled from table to table taking requests at restaurants, clubs, and private parties. It paid well, and we met hundreds of people. With some, we were able to share our faith in Jesus. Music and spirituality were no longer in conflict. Now they beautifully served the gospel. Music even played a pivotal role in introducing me to my future wife, Sally, who plays piano. But that's a story for another day.

We dissolved the trio after I graduated in 1976 and Roger and Linda headed to Japan to do missionary work. I married the following year. For the next nine years, I would manage Christian bookstores. That was certainly fulfilling the call to disseminate the Christian worldview. But my work schedule made free time scarce. Plus, I had become a father, welcoming a new child every few years. Because music performance is a jealous mistress, I had to set her aside to make time for spiritual inquiries and ongoing study. My guitar went into hibernation. Occasionally, it would emerge from its case for sing-alongs or to teach my kids "Pokey the Rodeo Clown," "Puff the Magic Dragon," and "Wild Thing." Within a few years, the kids were singing and playing the flute, drums, percussion, and guitar.

Over the years, we were pretty indiscriminate in our listening. The only criteria were "Is it edifying?" and "Does it build you up or tear you down?" Admittedly, I wasn't always sure. So Baroque composers such as Bach and Vivaldi would vie for our attention with not only Mozart, Beethoven, and Chopin but with classic rock from the Beatles, Motown, Cream, and the Eagles; the rural folk piano of George Winston; the neoclassical pop of Ray Lynch; and the New Orleans R&B piano of Professor Longhair. We listened to the jazz of Keith Jarrett, Thelonious Monk, and Dave Brubeck; popular Broadway musicals, including *Les Misérables* and *West Side Story*; and the signature songs of the great vocalists Sinatra, Eva Cassidy, Dean Martin, and Tony Bennett. As the kids got older, they'd share their favorite songs by Coldplay, John Mayer, Ben Rector, John Foreman, Red Hot Chili Peppers, Weezer, Foo Fighters, Mumford & Sons, Vulfpeck, Cake, the Lumineers, Bill Withers, and many others. Some took up swing dancing. Nick, James, and Evan all had bands that played ska-punk, indie rock, and reggae, and with their older sister Alexis and her husband, John, they eventually played music at Mass in their home parishes. Occasionally, we'd play together at home. Alexis, her friend Rachel, and I even scored and charted a medley of Beatles songs for two flutes and classical guitar, which we performed at a local pro-life dinner.

In general, though, I didn't feel free to play very much because a local Evangelical Charismatic congregation called me to be their pastor and the local Christian station asked me to host a daily talk program. I just grew too busy to play, but at least I was fulfilling my call to disseminate a Christian understanding of the world. Between the pulpit and the talk show, I was constantly reading, writing, speaking, and conducting interviews. There was no end to the stream of ideas and concepts. Even when our family came into full communion with the Catholic Church and I resigned the pastorate, I was preparing to launch what would become Ave Maria Radio. There was no time to work on my guitar playing.

So for nearly four decades, playing guitar was pushed into the corner of my life. This is not unusual. Many if not most men and women learn to say no to certain loves and passions because they are starting a business or trying to grow in their professional life. Their work demands more than eight hours a day. That was certainly the case with my apostolic work as well. So even though our home was flooded with great music, I had to content myself with listening.

As I grew older, my wife and now-adult kids urged me to take a break, relax a bit, maybe even get a hobby. I saw what they were saying. Even going to the movies or the Detroit Art Institute turned into a conversation about what I might be able to use on the radio. "Get out of your head and maybe do something with your hands" was the substance of their message. They urged me to pick up the guitar again. I was ambivalent. It had been so long. My dexterity and speed would be shot. I wanted to live with my fantasy about how good I once was. But with their gentle prodding, I agreed to wade into the shallow end of the pool, and one afternoon, with my sons James, Evan, and David, I bought an inexpensive, used electric guitar and a small amplifier. If I kept playing, maybe I'd graduate to a more serious—and expensive—instrument.

It felt good to take a small break from being a "vendor of words," as St. Augustine put it, and enjoy another aspect of human creativity. The Internet offered a wide range of tutorials. I began learning some classic rock solos, such as Eric Clapton's "Crossroads" and Santana's "El Farol." I'd chase down blues riffs from Mike Bloomfield and Johnny Winter's recordings. And jazz ballads and classics that I had enjoyed over the years, including "Autumn Leaves" and "Fly Me to the Moon" became part of my repertoire. Soon, I found myself complaining about the quality of the pickups, the action on the fretboard, and the tuning keys. So my son Nick borrowed different guitars from his friend Sam, who had played lead guitar in his old band. I liked all of Sam's guitars but couldn't bring myself to choose one. These instruments were expensive, after all, and we still had a son in high school. But a significant part of the delay was the reemergence of my old ambivalence about the way music distracted me from more "important," more "spiritual" duties. This time, however, Christ would resolve the tension between spirituality and music in my life. This is how.

On Christmas Day, 2019, Nick handed me an envelope with a picture of three classic electric guitars: a Les Paul, a Stratocaster, and a newer PRS Custom. Above the guitars was a command written in large font and bright colors: "Take your pick, BUT PICK ONE ALREADY!!" Inside the envelope was all the money I would need.

Over the next week, my family and I dawdled in music shops as I narrowed my choices. I finally settled on a beautiful semi-hollow PRS Custom SE. I was exultant and filled with gratitude for such a thoughtful gift. Those closest to me recognized one of the most persistent themes of my life and were now helping me develop it.

Yet some obsessive, nagging voice in the back of my head suggested I was just being self-indulgent. Intellectually, I knew this needling wasn't the Holy Spirit; it sounded more like the Accuser. Years before, I had discovered the difference between that neurotic nag and my properly formed conscience. But emotionally, it was annoying. To be melodramatic: "Who will deliver me from this pesky scrupulosity?"

As I was paying, the salesperson asked me to spell my name. Then, from somewhere to my right, I heard someone say: "Hey, Al! I thought that was you."

A middle-aged fellow whom I had never met before stepped up and shook my hand.

"Hi, I'm Joey Garcia," he said. "I've been listening to you since before you were a Catholic, and I'm still listening to you."

Joey was indeed an avid listener. He identified particular programs and themes that he loved. It was gratifying. He was a listener who "got" what my producer and I were trying to do on the program. Even after thirty years on the air, I remain grateful for all the encouragement and the generosity of spirit that listeners show me—even in unexpected places.

As Joey kept talking, my kids were amused at his enthusiasm but soon recognized that Joey was giving me a gift: a little kiss from my Heavenly Father.

Joey said: "I even love your bumper music. I've wondered if you played guitar because you choose some great cuts. Yeah, good ear. And here you are at Guitar Center. In fact, you should take that guitar and lay down some of your own tracks for bumper music." He even made bold to say: "That's why God's giving you this instrument. Enjoy it."

It was as though God, through Joey, had commanded, "Annoyance, be gone!" Joey Garcia had no idea that Christ was giving me reassurance through him. He became my brother of consolation that afternoon.

Many would see this as just a small thing. Why would God care about this hang-up in my interior life? Because I am His, and He wants me whole. Thanks to Joey, I can bear witness that this small moment revealed once again the tender affection of our Heavenly Father toward one of His children. The great God who counts the hairs of our head, calls us by name, and knows our inmost thoughts can be found in the magnificence of the big bang and in the smallest details of our lives. He is with us until the close of this age. In the meantime, let's see if I can get around to creating my own bumper music.

REFLECTIONS

—

FROM SCRIPTURE

*"O Lord, you have searched me and known me!
You know when I sit down and when I rise up;
you discern my thoughts from afar. You search
out my path and my lying down
and are acquainted with all my ways.
Even before a word is on my tongue,
behold, O Lord, you know it altogether.
You hem me in, behind and before,
and lay your hand upon me."*
(Psalm 139:1–5, ESV)

QUESTIONS

Spend some time meditating upon this
verse: "I came that they may have life and
have it abundantly" (John 10:10, ESV).
Is there something you enjoy,
something you feel called to do, but
have put aside due to the busyness
of life or some other reason?

Has a stranger, old friend, or loved
one ever given you a "nudge" that
confirmed the desire of your heart?

How might you be putting God in a box
and limiting His involvement in your life?

A Mission of Pilgrimage

BY JOHN HALE

WORDS OF WISDOM

Rise every morning excited for the gift of your life, trusting that God will give you His every grace for the day. Take a few moments to count each and every blessing. Then, commit to doing your best, and visualize yourself succeeding through the love and grace of God! Go forward, firmly trusting in Him and in His unfathomable love for you, knowing that you are firmly in His care.

SAINTLY ADVICE

"Do not fear what may happen tomorrow. The same loving Father who cares for you today will care for you tomorrow and every day. Either He will shield you from suffering, or He will give you unfailing strength to bear it. Be at peace, then, and put aside all anxious thoughts and imaginings." (St. Francis de Sales)

JOHN HALE is president and co-owner of Corporate Travel Service, a family-owned business founded in 1965 with the mission of transforming lives through travel and event experiences, including Catholic pilgrimages, educational tours, corporate events, music festivals on iconic stages worldwide, cultural tours, and cruises throughout the world. John has worked with numerous Fortune 500 companies, as well as the Vatican Museums, the Sistine Chapel Choir, school districts, archdioceses, parishes, universities, and various media outlets throughout the United States.

John graduated from the University of Michigan's LSA Honors Program and obtained his law degree from the University of Detroit Mercy School of Law. After graduating from law school, he clerked for Chief Justice Dorothy Comstock Riley on the Michigan Supreme Court. Following his clerkship, he was an associate attorney at Bodman and later served in the Office of the General Counsel at Ford Motor Company.

Currently, John serves on the board of directors of The Inn at St. John's, the Catholic Foundation of Michigan, and the Michigan Opera Theatre (where he also on the board of trustees). He chairs the Archdiocese of Detroit Advancement Council and the Michigan Chapter of the Patrons of the Arts in the Vatican Museums. John is a member of the Sovereign Military Hospitaller Order of St. John of Jerusalem, of Rhodes and of Malta, American Association; the Equestrian Order of the Holy Sepulchre of Jerusalem; and the Detroit chapter of Legatus. He and his wife, Kristan, have five children and reside in Michigan.

The COVID-19 pandemic has devastated the tour and travel industry and significantly disrupted our family's fifty-five-year-old travel business. Canceling thousands of cruises and tours, including pilgrimages, in the span of three months was extraordinarily difficult. It required me to live as never before with radical trust in God and His providence amid tremendous uncertainty.

International shutdowns and travel restrictions had significant and widespread consequences for our business, most of which could not be foreseen or easily remedied. There is true pain associated with the fear and reality of disappointing business partners around the world, beloved team members, and especially our clients. The continuous onslaught of bad news and draconian restrictions on movement mentally challenged us as we contemplated and worked to mitigate the consequences for our clients and our business.

Every day for months, more bad news for travel came. Early in the pandemic, two of the countries where we conduct most of our pilgrimages closed their borders. Next, cruise lines were ordered to cease operations, which ultimately required many of our large group cruises to be postponed for an entire year. After a series of challenging days, we hit a low point: the Oberammergau Passion Play was canceled. More than three years of steadfast work was suddenly extinguished along with the dreams of thousands of pilgrim clients. Every ten years, the play is performed to fulfill a promise made to God after He spared the village from, ironically, a seventeenth-century plague. In a five-hour performance on the impressive open-air stage of the Passion Play Theatre, more than two thousand participants—almost half the village—devotedly perform the story of Jesus of Nazareth from His entry into Jerusalem to His death and resurrection.

One of the most difficult aspects of the COVID-19 crisis has been the uncertainty over how long it will last. Easily fearing and even at times despairing for the future can distort reality and compromise our trust in God and His plan for us.

The mission of our travel business has always been to enhance lives and promote culture through thoughtfully produced travel experiences. One of the primary ways in which we execute this mission is by organizing pilgrimages to places of religious significance, such as the Holy Land, Rome, and the Marian shrines of Fatima and Lourdes. Led by the Holy Spirit, our team organizes each pilgrimage with detailed care and consideration to move each pilgrim closer to the heart of Christ. When planning, the team considers the four pillars of pilgrimage that we believe create the environment in which the Holy Spirit most profoundly moves: (1) disconnecting from daily routines, (2) engaging with sacred places visited, (3) receiving the sacraments through daily Mass and Confession, and (4) developing opportunities for the relationships among pilgrims to flourish.

These pilgrimages have been a priority for me as a Catholic sincerely pursuing my Faith. I don't just want to sell someone a trip: I want each pilgrim to have an encounter with God. Many pilgrims have shared with me their moving experiences and their sense that God was speaking to them personally. God has certainly led people to Himself through these pilgrimages. Almost weekly, our team is inspired by our clients' stories of healing, of faith renewed and relationships restored. And we respond, "All praise to God," because we are deeply convicted that although God has called us to this mission, the work is His, and we are His unworthy but grateful servants.

When our mission abruptly ran into the cement wall that was the pandemic, each of us, in his own way, has been tempted to question his ability to carry out this work. I kept asking, "When and how will our ability to execute our mission be restored, Lord?" Even so, we have received many affirmations, and clearly, God has been working through many people to provide each of us consolation and support.

My most astounding affirmation of my mission came during a Mass celebrating one of my patron saints, St. John the Baptist. St. John is also the patron of the Order of Malta, a lay religious order devoted to serving the sick and the poor. Every June, on St. John's feast day, members of the Michigan Area of the Order of Malta gather to celebrate Mass.

At Mass, especially during the Consecration, I was asking God, in light of what was happening in the world and all the uncertainty, what my mission was. As I asked God to reveal His plan for my mission, the moment I thought the word "mission," Monsignor said the word "pilgrim." He was praying the Third Eucharistic Prayer, which contains these words: "May this sacrifice, which has made our peace with you, advance the peace and salvation of all the world. Strengthen in faith and love your pilgrim Church on earth."

The simultaneity of the words "mission" and "pilgrim" was overwhelming. I could hardly believe it. I felt a deep sense of peace that God was providing for me and answering my prayers. I recalled learning how the Holy Spirit provides for us at every moment, if only to carry us to the next. We have the responsibility to create an atmosphere in which we can hear the Holy Spirit and allow Him to act in and through us. This requires three things: belief that God acts through the power of the Holy Spirit; the quieting of our souls; and gratitude for the moments when we realize the Holy Spirit is acting.

The pandemic felt like a temporary halt to my mission, but it became the means through which God spoke directly to me, comforted me, and gave me *certainty* about my mission at this time.

REFLECTIONS

FROM SCRIPTURE

"Consider it all joy, my brothers, when you encounter various trials, for you know that the testing of your faith produces perseverance. And let perseverance be perfect, so that you may be perfect and complete, lacking in nothing. But if any of you lacks wisdom, he should ask God who gives to all generously and ungrudgingly, and he will be given it. But he should ask in faith, not doubting, for the one who doubts is like a wave of the sea that is driven and tossed about by the wind." (James 1:2–6, NABRE)

QUESTIONS

Are you overly reminiscent and preoccupied with the past, or so fearful of the future that you are unable to see the blessings of the present?

Do you read Scripture daily and meditatively to allow God's Word to penetrate your soul, your life, and your very being, such that you see His actions and hear His guidance in your life?

Do you quiet your soul throughout each day to unite your intentions, fears, and anxieties to the love of God the Father and God the Son, which is God the Holy Spirit?

17

In the Darkness of Night, "Here I Am, Lord"

BY STEVE RAY ("JERUSALEM JONES")

WORDS OF WISDOM

All of us have something God expects us to do. He may surprise us when we're least anticipating it and when we feel the least capable. It's often at such moments that He requires us to do the biggest things in our lives. We will either say no and turn away or realize our own inadequacies and trust Him to enable us to do what He requires.

SAINTLY ADVICE

"God does not require that we be successful, only that we be faithful." (Mother Teresa)

STEVE RAY was born in 1954 to parents who had just become Christians through a Billy Graham Crusade. He was raised in a Fundamentalist Baptist family and in 1976 married Janet, who came from a long line of Protestants. On Pentecost Sunday, 1994, they both converted to Catholicism. Steve began writing a letter to his father explaining why they became Catholic. This letter soon became the book *Crossing the Tiber: Evangelical Protestants Discover the Historic Church*, published by Ignatius Press. Steve's passions are writing, speaking, producing Catholic films, and leading pilgrimages to biblical lands. Steve and Janet have been to the Holy Land over 170 times, exploring, filming, and leading thousands of pilgrims. Steve is a regular guest on Catholic radio and TV, appearing on Catholic Answers, Ave Maria Radio, Relevant Radio, and EWTN. He also writes Bible studies for Catholic Scripture Study International. Visit Steve at CatholicConvert.com.

I grabbed my wife in her deep sleep and started to blurt out what I had just seen. Janet listened in disbelief and, with what could be interpreted as a bit of frustration, mumbled that I was crazy and should go back to sleep. She promptly rolled over with a few deep breaths and went back to sleep. She didn't even realize that I jumped out of bed and never returned that night.

It all started when we first visited the Holy Land and completely fell under its spell. No member of our young family was untouched by the sacramental nature of the land. The whole time, we felt we had to remove our shoes to stand on this holy ground. The moment we stepped off the plane, I knelt down on the tarmac to weep. We wept at every holy site. When the priest asked me to read at Mass, I tried for a full minute to swallow the lump in my throat and wipe the tears from my eyes before finally giving up and returning to my seat.

When we returned home from that pilgrimage, we thought about how marvelous it would be to take all Catholics to Israel to experience it as we had. Of course, that was not possible, but the thought had been planted in our hearts.

That night, something happened that I had never experienced before and haven't since. It was after midnight; Janet and I were sound asleep. The curtains were drawn, and the room was so dark you couldn't see your hand in front of your face if you tried. Suddenly, I bolted awake from a deep sleep. I grabbed Janet's shoulders, shook her awake, and blurted out what I had seen. She was shaking with shock and fear. Was the house on fire? Was I having a heart attack? "What are you talking about?" she asked.

I took a deep breath and started over.

"We have to make a video documentary on the Bible and the story of salvation history from a Catholic perspective!"

What inspired my outburst is still not clear. We discussed it often. Was it an angel that awakened me? Maybe a dream or night vision? I jokingly say it might have been indigestion. But one thing I am certain of is that in the middle of the night, God put an idea in my mind that was so compelling it woke me up instantly—it was all there in my head.

Still shaking, my wife said: "We have to do *what*? We can't even take good pictures; how does God expect us to make movies? You are crazy; go back to sleep!"

Janet did go back to sleep, but I hopped out of bed. In the morning, she found me feverishly typing on my computer. I had to get everything on paper before the vision, impulse, infusion—whatever it was—vanished from my mind. It consumed my whole day. The outline for the series flowed from my mind through my fingers and onto the screen. The titles of the videos, the sites to be filmed, the truths to be expressed—they were all there, crystal clear.

Had that been the end of it all, I could've chalked it up to indigestion and hyperventilation, but twenty years later, the *Footprints of God* film series is almost finished (nine out of ten have been completed as of this writing). The films have been enthusiastically received and shown around the world in homes, churches, schools, and seminaries, and on television. They have influenced many lives, and they made our dream come true: through the *Footprints of God* series, we have taken people to the Holy Land, so to speak, and helped them love and understand the truth of the Bible and the Church on location.

I write this not to toot my own horn, but to bring glory to God, who took two people with no training in filmmaking, no money, and no idea what they were getting into. He woke us up in the middle of the night with something so radical that any rational person would disregard it as a crazy idea. He gave us the marvelous support and funding of Ignatius Press, and with one miracle after another, He made the whole midnight vision a reality.

My story just goes to show what can happen when we say yes to God. We thank God as He continues to smile down on us—His humble, surprised, and grateful servants.

REFLECTIONS

———

FROM SCRIPTURE

"After he had finished speaking, he said to Simon, 'Put out into deep water and lower your nets for a catch.' Simon said in reply, 'Master, we have worked hard all night and have caught nothing, but at your command I will lower the nets.' When they had done this, they caught a great number of fish and their nets were tearing." (Luke 5:4–6, NABRE)

———

QUESTIONS

Scripture informs us that God communicates with His people in special ways. Are you open to the way God speaks to you?

Notice the way many of God's people have responded to Him when He communicates with them—they are quick to reply, "Here I am" (see Gen. 22:1; Exod. 3:4; and 1 Sam. 3:4). Are you prepared to respond in the same manner at any moment?

What are some issues that may keep God from speaking to us or prevent us from hearing Him?

Looking back, can you identify a time when God may have spoken to you? If so, how did you respond? What might you have done differently?

Faith, Family, and Friends

BY JOAN LEWIS

WORDS OF WISDOM

Sometimes, a heart has to be broken to heal. Throughout my life, my parents have had more words of healing and comfort and love than anyone else. Their strong faith and love got all of us through tough times, especially great disappointments and health issues.

SAINTLY ADVICE

"Unless there is a Good Friday in your life, there can be no Easter Sunday!" (Venerable Fulton J. Sheen)

"I know God won't give me anything I can't handle! I just wish he didn't trust me so much!" (St. Teresa of Calcutta)

"Be not afraid." (St. John Paul II)

JOAN LEWIS, after years of teaching French in the United States, moved to Rome forty years ago and has worked for or covered the Vatican as a journalist in that time. Fluent in several languages, Joan was a member of several high-level Holy See delegations to international conferences (Cairo in 1994, Copenhagen in 1995, Beijing in 1995, Istanbul in 1996, and Doha in 2004). She covered numerous papal trips, one papal funeral, one papal resignation, two conclaves, and the canonizations of John XXIII, John Paul II, Teresa of Calcutta, and Paul VI. She is the author of several books. In 2005, Pope Benedict named her a Dame of St. Sylvester. She is also a Lady of the Order of the Holy Sepulchre and a Dame of the Constantinian Order.

She retired from the Vatican in June 2005 and was appointed EWTN's first Rome bureau chief that fall. She hosts the weekly show *Vatican Insider* on EWTN. Read her daily blog, *Joan's Rome*, at joansrome.wordpress.com. Follow her on Facebook at www.facebook.com/joan.lewis.10420 and @JoansRome on Twitter.

Faith, family, and friends.

Those three words will certainly be a good title if I ever write my autobiography. They are brilliant threads that, when woven together, produce a beautiful tapestry depicting a life I could only call wondrous.

I was blessed to be born into a loving and large family. I had my wonderful mom and dad, my sister Gail, my brothers Bill and Dick, very special grandparents, sixteen aunts and uncles, and dozens of first cousins. The Catholic Faith was one of the ties that bound us together. Be it a birthday, anniversary, wedding, or graduation, we loved any reason to get together and have fun and laugh until it hurt. Even at funerals, as we reminisced about the life of the deceased, we always seemed to find a reason for laughter amid our tears.

Growing up, I both assumed and hoped that this would be my life: a happy marriage, children, a large extended family. This was a common dream in those years, more common than hopes for a career-oriented life.

But God had other plans. As it turned out, a career, not marriage, seemed to be on my horizon. I became a working gal. French was my major in college, and as a French teacher for many years, I brought students overseas on study tours and eventually realized a second dream: moving to Italy. The tapestry of my life now included another thread—journalism—as I ended up both writing about and working for the Vatican.

Then, one day, someone from my past entered my life and filled it with love and wonder. To make a long story short, I moved back to America to get married and finally fulfill my first dream. But again, God had other plans. So did my fiancé!

With the help of faith, family, and friends, I got through the devastation of lost love. After six months of heartbreak and tears, I simply turned to God one day, raised my eyes to heaven, and said, "Okay, Lord, my life is in Your hands!"

God had always been part of my life, but I had never turned my entire life over to Him. In that moment, in an inexplicable way, I could hear God laughing! He was rejoicing at my decision, and, as I soon learned, He intended to fill my life with His plans!

Those God-filled moments, those Godcidences, have been count-less ever since. The family that the Lord has given me is bigger than any I could have created through a loving marriage. My biological family ties are still many: nine nieces and nephews, twenty-six grand-nieces and grandnephews, and only the Lord knows how many total cousins! But my God-given extended family is as numerous as the stars in a galaxy. I have been blessed to have in my life countless priests and seminarians (my adopted sons) from around the world. I have friends and families on six continents as a result of my years at the Vatican. Through my blog and books and my world travels, I have met and shared amazing times with fellow Catholics and Christians—people who have become like family to me.

At every corner I have turned in these years—be it in Chicago, Saigon, or Cairo; Budapest, Beijing, or Istanbul; the Holy Land or Maryland—the Lord has been there, tapping me on the shoulder and saying, "Joan, here is a new member of your family."

Each tap on the shoulder, each new face, each encounter in life, each new thread of that tapestry was all part of God's blueprint for my spiritual family. These moments were never just coincidences: they were God's moments, Godcidences.

REFLECTIONS

—

FROM SCRIPTURE

*"Peace I leave with you; my peace
I give you. I do not give to you as
the world gives. Do not let your
hearts be troubled and do not be
afraid."* (John 14:27, NIV)

"The Lord *is close to the brokenhearted
and saves those who are crushed
in spirit."* (Psalm 34:18, NIV)

*"He heals the brokenhearted
and binds up their wounds."*
(Psalm 147:3, NIV)

QUESTIONS

What role did your family play
in the growth of your faith?
Do they still have a role?

Do you have enough faith to
turn your life over to God?

Are you able to recognize when
God speaks to you? Are you open to
listening? Often, His answers to our
prayers come in the form of a person,
an event, or maybe something you read
or heard that He sent into your life.

19

Redemption and Hope in Marriage

BY JULIE ALEXANDER

WORDS OF WISDOM

*No matter how much pain you feel or how deeply
you are hurting, there is always an opportunity for
redemption when you center your marriage on Christ.*

SAINTLY ADVICE

*"Love is never something ready made, something merely
'given' to man and woman, it is always at the same time a
'task' which they are set. Love should be seen as something
which in a sense never 'is' but is always only 'becoming,' and
what it becomes depends upon the contribution of both persons
and the depth of their commitment."* (Pope John Paul II)[13]

[13] *Love and Responsibility* (San Francisco: Ignatius Press, 1993), 139.

JULIE AND GREG ALEXANDER are authors, speakers, Marriage Disciples, and co-founders of the Alexander House Apostolate (www.thealexanderhouse.org). They co-wrote *Marriage 911: How God Saved Our Marriage (and Can Save Yours, Too)* and *40 Days of Growing in Love Through Prayer*. The Alexanders also co-hosted the EWTN series *Marriage Works in Christ* and have their own weekly podcast, *Greg and Julie: Your Marriage Disciples*. Greg and Julie have over twenty years of experience working with and helping other couples and share their expertise whenever they can. They have been featured speakers at many conferences and are frequent guests on Catholic radio. Greg and Julie have been married since July 1987. They have four sons, three daughters, four grandsons, and a granddaughter.

Greg called me into the room and said: "No wonder we are messing it up! We are not even coming close to living marriage the way God intended."

I was dazed and confused. We had just ripped our children's hearts out with the news that we were going to get a divorce. Their little seven- and nine-year-old bodies were huddled in the corner, and they were crying their eyes out, shaking, holding each other together. All the while, our hearts had grown stone cold as we thought only of being free from the misery and hurt and pain we had carried for so long.

"Create in me a clean heart, O God," David sings in Psalm 51. This is what God did for us. Our purification began with the simple proclamation: "God has a plan for marriage. Listen to what our beautiful Church has to say about this sacrament." My heart was on fire, and the disgust and resentment I had stored up in the recesses of my heart began to burn away. I felt a warmth come over me that could be explained only as the loving arms of our Father, reaching down from the heavens to embrace me.

When we stopped hiding behind the facade of "everything is fine with us," we were able to sift through the wreckage of our tattered hearts and wounded spirits. It seemed as if a burden were lifted once we began divulging our brokenness to our children and a few family members. We had done everything you could do wrong in a marriage; you could say we had "no love left," but that was because we had a misconception of what love was. We began to realize that love was not a feeling but an act of the will: something that you have to choose to do every minute of every day. Our marriage had not been established on the foundation of Jesus Christ but on the shifting sand of emotions, lust, selfishness, pride, and worldly success.

I still recall the moment that Greg called me into the room. My heart sank when he yelled my name, but amid my instant feeling of concern, I noticed his voice had an unfamiliar tone. This wasn't the tone I was used to hearing when we lamented our anger, frustration, and mutual contempt, when we spoke about the discoveries of our unfaithfulness and deceitful practices.

I approached the doorway of our bedroom. Greg seemed to have a softer look in his eyes; he actually appeared to have a sense of care and concern for me. As I sat down, he started to share the truths that he had uncovered about the Sacrament of Marriage, and I immediately felt a spark in the depths of my soul. Yes, my heart was on fire for him, for my husband—the man I promised to love and to cherish and to accompany until death do us part. For the first time, I felt real love for this man. I was like a sponge as he poured his newfound knowledge over me. There was a hopeful rush that caressed my heart, and I wanted to know where to go from here.

"This is incredible," I said to Greg. "What do we do now?"

He looked deep into my eyes, and it felt as if he were peering into my soul.

"I think we need to pray," he said.

He grabbed my hand and fell to his knees, pulling me with him. He began to say a prayer from his heart: "Heavenly Father, we have tried living our marriage the way we think it should be lived, and that has not worked. We have also tried living our marriage by the ways of the world, and that has not worked either. Heavenly Father, right here, right now, we sincerely ask you to come into our lives and show us how you want us to live this thing called marriage. If you deliver us from this evil, we will commit the rest of our lives to working in some type of marriage or family ministry."

Well, God went to work, and so did we. Within a week, we had both resigned from our corporate jobs. Indeed, this was grace. We knew that we did not want to let anything stand in the way of allowing God to fill us with His grace and His mercy, and we wanted to stay committed to the promise we made. Our jobs provided the income that allowed us to get involved in all kinds of things that were not in line with the direction we needed to go. For years, our lives had been upside down and our priorities out of order: work came first, then money, because it provided for all of the "stuff" that we felt we needed. Then came our children, other people, our marriage, and God at the very bottom. Back then, when all hell would break loose and we realized how miserable we were, we would turn to God and ask why He was allowing our lives to be such a mess. I mean, it had nothing to do with us, right?

Quitting our jobs was the first hurdle to clear. We did not know what we were going to do, but Greg could not stop studying. He was devouring the Church's teachings, Scripture, and the *Catechism* and gleaning all he could about the Sacrament of Marriage. Our distant ships passing in the night were all of a sudden docked at the same port, and our conversations became never-ending. We would stay up all night discussing our discoveries and praying for guidance from the Holy Spirit.

We started to see clearly that our lack of knowledge (Hosea 4:6) had caused us to perish. We had become so far removed from any semblance of what a holy marriage should reflect. At that point, we were married and living single lives; we had spiritually divorced each other. We chose instead to replace money and professional success with the one thing that started to matter most in our lives: a relationship with Jesus Christ. We realized we had to become an example to our children and the rest of the world. It felt as if God were sending us on a mission.

While Greg was getting dressed one morning, he heard an internal voice say, "I want you to speak to my people." Overwhelmed by the experience, he fell to his knees and asked, "What do you mean speak to your people?" He sensed the presence of God in his heart and knew that God was calling him to do something. Then, he heard the words "You need to pray and go to Confession."

Greg couldn't make any sense of this. He went to see a priest, who challenged us to go back and study and told us, "If God is calling you to do His work, you must remain a clean vessel, and you have to stay in communication with Him to know what He wants you to do."

It was evident that we were to shed our old wineskins and turn from our wicked ways by becoming new wineskins, filled with the new wine of God. Scripture tells us that old wineskins cannot contain new wine; they will burst, and the wine will spill (Matt. 9:14-17).

Our lives and our marriage were becoming a new creation as we started to learn about having a relationship with Christ. St. Jerome said it best: "Ignorance of Scripture is ignorance of Christ." So we figured we needed to continue reading and praying with Scripture. Before, we did not truly understand that Christ died for us on the Cross, nor did we ever so much as open the Bible. It was as if a light came on when we understood what it meant that the Word became flesh and dwelt among us. Jesus Christ is God in the flesh. He came not only to share our humanity but to free us from sin. Wow!

We felt like eagles soaring in the sky and riding on the currents of grace. Greg was studying everything he could get his hands on about the Sacrament of Marriage. At the same time, he increasingly wanted to know more about this Catholic Faith that we inherited but did not understand. We experienced our most significant breakthrough when Greg focused his studies on the Sacrament of Reconciliation. He revisited the things he learned as a youth: when you go to Confession, you receive absolution for your mortal sins, and you feel a burden lifted from your heart. All of this is true, but that day, Greg was taken deeper into the meaning of the sacrament.

As he finished his studies for the day, he closed his notebook and heard a voice saying, "Those things are true, but that should not be the reason you go to the sacrament."

Greg looked around the room to see where this voice was coming from, but seeing no one, he responded internally, "What else is there?"

In an instant, the voice responded, "You should go to Confession because you have come to understand that because of your actions, you have severed your relationship with your Heavenly Father, and your immediate desire should be to repair that relationship."

For whatever reason, that made total sense to Greg. He called me into the room, explained what happened, and assured me that he was not going crazy. Then, he said, "We need to go to the Sacrament of Reconciliation."

Greg and I conducted an in-depth examination of conscience, grabbed our notes, and went to celebrate the Sacrament of Reconciliation. After leaving the confessional, Greg stated that he knew that this whole "grace thing" was real: before Confession, he still had many issues to deal with concerning our past, but afterward, they were gone. All he felt was a desire to work on our marriage and to love me the way I deserved.

We started reflecting on the daily readings, going deeper into prayer, and outlining the changes we needed to make in our lives. At this point, our Faith became more than just going to Mass on Sundays: it became part of daily life. A burning desire replaced our apathy about having to check Sunday Mass off our to-do list for the week. We began to get involved in the life of the Church. We were in awe of the ways God spoke to us in different circumstances. The more we read and studied, the more we transformed our lives and oriented our hearts to the truth. Living in accordance with God's plan gave us a joy we never thought possible. God became the focal point of our lives and our marriage, and yes, life was awesome.

We started praying together in the morning and again before bed. Our intimacy grew as we invited God into our union. We were not battling against each other anymore; we were two becoming one, working together toward a common goal—heaven!

God helped us fulfill our promise to serve Him in marriage and family ministry. One day, we received a call from the diocese asking if we could fill in for a temporary position in the Family Life Office. That temporary position lasted two and a half years.

Shortly after we started working in the Family Life Office, Greg found a hidden treasure on the bookshelf: Pope Paul VI's Encyclical Letter *Humanae Vitae*. It was an eye-opener. After reading a few pages, Greg felt compelled to give me a call.

"Are you sitting down?" he asked.

I became anxious, wondering what he was going to say.

Then, he told me: "Julie, we have a problem. I had no idea that getting a vasectomy was against the Church's teachings or God's plan for our marriage. I need to go to Confession."

A few days later, we received a flyer in the mail from my mom about a marriage conference in Denver. We decided to go. When we arrived at the conference, we found ourselves sitting in the front row with my brother and sister-in-law. They were the only two in my family who knew about Greg's vasectomy.

The first speaker, a priest, presented a talk on God's plan for marriage. We were like proud peacocks with our chests stuck out, because everything he covered was exactly what we were learning and incorporating in our marriage. But the second talk hit us like a ton of bricks. Presenting one of his very first talks on the Theology of the Body was a gentleman by the name of Christopher West. He spoke about how listening to the messages of society, especially its encouragement of contraception and sterilization, causes us to twist God's plan for sex.

The more he talked, the more we sank in our seats. We were not so thrilled to be sitting in the front row anymore. Mr. West closed his talk by asking if anyone present had undergone sterilization. If so, he suggested that person repent and prayerfully consider reversing the procedure.

Our drive back to Austin was quiet and reflective. Greg said he felt a stirring in his heart. We went to God in prayer and asked Him to give us a sign if He wanted us to consider reversing Greg's vasectomy.

The following Monday, while thumbing through the books on the office shelf, I came across a tiny booklet, *Physicians Healed*, published by One More Soul, a pro-life apostolate in Ohio. The booklet contained a compilation of stories written by doctors who used to prescribe the Pill and perform vasectomies and tubal ligations. They shared how they decided to live their Faith while practicing life-giving medicine instead of engaging in activities that are contrary to God's plan for marriage and family. On the back of the booklet was a sticker indicating that it was a gift from the director of the Natural Family Planning Office.

I picked up the phone, called the director, and said: "Hi, my name is Julie Alexander, and my husband and I are new in the Family Life Office. I was wondering if you by chance have any information for people who might come into our office looking for doctors who perform reversal?"

The director gave us the names and numbers of three doctors: two in Austin and one in New Braunfels. We left messages with the two in Austin, but the doctor in New Braunfels answered the phone. Nervously, I asked if he had any info on his vasectomy reversal procedure. I was quick to mention that I was asking in case someone came to our office wanting this type of information. The doctor gave me the name of his website, asked for the address of our office, and promised to mail me information about the procedure.

Greg immediately pulled up the doctor's website. He was inspired by the Scripture verses and images of "post-reversal" babies. After a few moments, Greg asked me to call the doctor back. I was a bit confused and asked why. He insisted that this was the doctor who would reverse his vasectomy. Then, Greg discovered that the procedure would cost anywhere from $6,000 to $20,000. That was the sign we'd prayed for. It had to be, because we had no money left. In fact, after quitting our jobs and working part-time for the Church, we had only $500 in our checking account.

But Greg wouldn't accept any excuses and ask me to call back for an appointment. So I called again, and the receptionist answered. I asked if we could make an appointment to see the doctor.

Before I could take a breath, she responded, "I have a cancellation for tomorrow at eleven-thirty; can you all make it?"

"We'll be there," I said.

The doctor seemed surprised to see us that morning.

"Greg and Julie Alexander ... Julie, didn't I just talk to you on the phone yesterday?" he asked. "What's wrong—is the mail not fast enough?"

I confessed that we were seeking information for ourselves. We told him our story of being on the brink of divorce, coming to realize that we had made a huge mistake, and now not feeling comfortable working in marriage ministry. The doctor treated us with total compassion in our brokenness. He shared with us his conversion story and then took us on a tour of his facility. He explained the procedure; we saw the equipment, and as we walked backed to his office, we passed the wall where the pictures of reversal babies were displayed.

I could see the connection between the doctor and Greg. When the doctor finally asked for our thoughts, Greg responded without hesitation: "I want you to do this. When can it happen?"

Looking through his calendar, the doctor replied: "I have a spot next Tuesday at seven-thirty. Can you make it?"

Greg, in his excitement, shouted, "Sign me up—I'll take it."

I did not want to ruin the moment, but one of us had to be the realist in this situation. I shared with the good doctor that I believed in his abilities to perform this procedure. Still, I had to be perfectly honest and tell him that we knew the costs associated with a vasectomy reversal. I timidly stated that there was no way we could afford the procedure unless he was willing to arrange some sort of payment plan. He leaned back in his chair and looked up at the ceiling for a quick moment; then, he leaned forward and said: "You know, I think the world of you two. Not only about where you have been, but where you are going. I tell you what: I want to invest in your ministry. Come and see me next Tuesday and bring me $500."

Again, that was the last $500 we had, but we were not going to let that stand between God and us and keep Greg from returning to the way God created him.

The operation was a success. The doctor warned us that the time between the vasectomy and the reversal meant we had about only a 20 percent chance of ever conceiving again. That was okay with us. We just wanted to be right with God again, and if we were to conceive, that would be a bonus.

I guess the doctor knew what he was doing because we conceived not only once but five times. As of this writing, we have seven children and four grandsons and a granddaughter. The miraculous grace of repenting and not only believing but living the good news has been incredible. Once we turned back to God and invited Him to be a part of our sacred union, He took our mess and made it a message to share with the whole world. And so, for the past twenty years, we have been proclaiming the beauty, goodness, and truth of God's plan for marriage!

REFLECTIONS

FROM SCRIPTURE

"Be kind to one another,
compassionate, forgiving one another
as God has forgiven you in Christ."
(Ephesians 4:32, NABRE)

QUESTIONS

How do you celebrate God
in your marriage?

Are you willing to surrender your
idea of marriage and ask the Holy
Spirit to guide you on a new path
toward God's plan for marriage?

Do you read Scripture with your spouse?

Are you willing to be servant-spouses,
serving God through each other?

Have you ever thought about the moment
when you will see God face-to-face and

He will ask you how well you cared
for His son or daughter in this life?

How often do you thank
God for your spouse?

Do you complain about or celebrate
the differences in your marriage?

Have you thought about writing out a
plan for how you as a couple and as a
family will honor God in your lives?

Do you ever encourage each other to
go to God for direction or answers?

Our Lady's Guiding Hand

BY GAIL CONIGLIO

WORDS OF WISDOM

Sometimes our crosses can be our heaviest burdens, but they can become lighter once we hold God's hand and allow Our Lady to accompany us, just as she did with Jesus on the road to Calvary. God can use everything for His good, no matter how difficult it is initially. Mary is always there for us, and she is our gentle Mother, calling us and leading us to her Son, Jesus. Don't underestimate the power of praying the Rosary. If we are open to God, He will be there for us, and our hearts will sing praises to Him, which will in turn become music to our ears.

SAINTLY ADVICE

"More tears are shed over answered prayers than unanswered ones." (St. Teresa of Avila)

"Pray as though everything depended on God. Work as though everything depended on you." (St. Augustine)

GAIL CONIGLIO has been working in Catholic marketing and media for over eighteen years, serving as marketing consultant, literary agent, and publicist for several Catholic media personalities, including Fr. Mitch Pacwa, S.J., and Teresa Tomeo. She earned a bachelor's degree in marketing from the University of Florida and began her work in Catholic lay evangelization while serving in both the Charismatic and Cursillo movements. Gail earned a certificate of evangelization from the Archdiocese of Miami.

Gail is an active parishioner and has been a small-group study leader for Women of Grace, a catechist, and an RCIA teacher. With Tomeo, Gail co-authored the study guide companion to Tomeo's *Beyond Sunday: Becoming a 24/7 Catholic*. She served as a host for the American Chamber of Christians in Business show *Chamber Hour*. Prior to that, she worked in sales and marketing in the hospitality industry. She served on the board of directors of the Hospitality Sales and Marketing Association International and the National Association of Catering Executives in Broward County. She received numerous awards from both organizations. Connect with Gail on Twitter and LinkedIn @GailConiglio.

In the Great Jubilee Year 2000, I began leading a four-year study at my parish, St. Mark the Evangelist Catholic Church. The study focused on Pope St. John Paul II's writings, including *Mulieris Dignitatem* ("On the Dignity and Vocation of Women") and *Redemptoris Mater* ("Mother of theRedeemer"). I specifically remember praying before the study began, asking God to increase my love and devotion to the Blessed Virgin Mary. I asked Jesus to draw me closer to His Mother. I was a mother of two beautiful children, Anthony and Courtney, and I knew in my heart that I needed to imitate Our Lady if I wanted to grow in holiness. The Lord really opened my eyes to the dignity of women and our proper role in society. I learned so much and was amazed by how Our Lady pondered so many things in her heart and by her profound trust and receptivity of God's will in her life. She was a wonderful inspiration for me, and my heart desired to continue to grow in my relationship with her and her Son.

In summer 2002, during our family trip to Orlando, we went to Sunday Mass on our last day of our vacation at the Basilica of the National Shrine of Mary, Queen of the Universe. Little did I know that we were there on the feast of the Queenship of Mary—the namesake of the shrine! After Mass, I was drawn to the shrine's side chapel, which had a beautiful mosaic of Our Lady of Guadalupe and St. Juan Diego. When I had learned that Our Lady of Guadalupe was the only apparition in which Mary was with child, I prayed to her that I would have a third child.

On our way home in the car, I felt a strong desire to put a statue of Our Lady in our front yard to honor her and to thank her for always helping me. The very next day, my next-door neighbor knocked on my door and said: "Gail, I have been meaning to ask you something for a while and I keep forgetting. I have had a statue of the Blessed Virgin Mary sitting in my garage for over ten years, and I really want to give it away to someone that would want it—would you like it?"

I couldn't believe my ears! I started crying, overwhelmed with joy that Our Lady was there all this time waiting for me to open my heart to her. I continued to pray to Our Lady of Guadalupe for another child, and I soon became pregnant with my daughter Gianna. She was born in September 2004, and I chose Marie as her middle name in honor of Our Blessed Mother. The summer after that, we went back to Orlando to the same shrine, and I brought my daughter Gianna into the same chapel and knelt down with tears of gratitude. From then on, I started to pray the Rosary more frequently.

The very next year, my son Anthony was diagnosed with type 1 diabetes at age nine. Of my three children, Anthony had the greatest difficulty with getting immunization shots at the doctor's office. Every time I took him to the doctor, he would ask if he had to get a shot. You could imagine how devastated we were upon learning he would have to give himself four shots a day! I remember the day he asked me: "So, Mommy, when is this diabetes thing going away? I really don't like these shots and can't wait until I get better."

Holding back tears, I had to explain gently that diabetes was a lifelong condition. It is not easy seeing your child suffer, and it was then that I realized that Our Blessed Mother knows this best. Looking back, I now see and truly believe that the Lord knew I would need a closer relationship to His Mother in order to get through this trying time. Having to get up in the middle of the night to test Anthony's blood sugar and having to measure and weigh his every morsel of food were real challenges. God sent me to that study at St.

Mark's to help prepare me for this time so that I could better support Anthony as he struggled to accept having diabetes. He was on a specific type of insulin regimen that required him to eat a certain amount of carbohydrates at specific times, even if he wasn't hungry. As Anthony's struggle continued, I decided to enroll him in piano lessons to get his mind off the diabetes. He began playing on a small piano keyboard with sixty-one keys. His elementary school music teacher, Mr. Michael Rowe, generously gave Anthony an old piano he had been storing in his basement, so that he could play with a full set of eighty-eight keys. Anthony progressed very quickly. Within six months, he learned and memorized George Gershwin's fifteen-minute solo-piano version of *Rhapsody in Blue*. He was progressing so quickly that his piano teacher told him he needed a better piano if he wanted to improve his technique. Anthony told me that he was going to start praying his Rosary specifically for Mary's help finding an affordable high-end piano.

During Easter break 2009, we went to my dear friend Mary Rose's home to swim in her pool. Anthony was telling her about his prayers to Our Lady for a new piano. Mary Rose said: "Anthony, I don't know when or how, but I am confident that God has already picked out a beautiful piano for you. It may be one year or ten years from now, but keep the faith, and God will answer your prayer."

Two months later, we went to Alabama to celebrate Fr. Mitch Pacwa's thirtieth ordination anniversary, as I was doing marketing work for his Jesuit apostolate, Ignatius Productions. On that trip, during a celebration dinner, Ignatius Productions board member Phillip Rumore and his wife, Carole, announced that they would like to work on getting Anthony a new piano. They told us it was their joy to help Anthony improve his piano skills, and they bought him a brand new Yamaha piano, which arrived at our doorstep four months later, exactly three years to the day that Anthony began taking piano lessons. Just two months afterward, Anthony won second place in one of the most prestigious piano competitions in Florida, the Music Teachers National Association (MTNA) Florida State Piano Competition. The lady running the competition asked Anthony which other competitions he had participated in. We explained this was his first major one. She was shocked and said to us that this was a miracle, because she had never heard of anyone, let alone someone with just three years of experience, whose first major competition was the MTNA competition at Florida State.

I later realized how much Our Lady had helped us along the way. It was Anthony's diagnosis that led him to music, which helped him to heal. The piano taught him discipline, and he seemed to advance even further academically, especially in mathematics, as he played increasingly difficult pieces of music. He would explain to me that the complex organization of harmony and rhythm in these pieces was, in fact, very mathematical. He accomplished so much as a musician that he was invited to audition at the college level at both the Juilliard School and the Manhattan School of Music. He ended up accepting a full scholarship to Indiana University's Jacobs School of Music, where he was blessed to study under renowned Grammy Award–winning pianist André Watts.

Anthony was able to test out of almost all his music theory courses, as well as several other classes, which allowed him to earn four bachelor's degrees (music, mathematics, physics, and astronomy/astrophysics) within four years. Plus, he even took a semester to study music overseas in Vienna, Austria, and in his senior year was awarded the prestigious Churchill Scholarship, which afforded him the opportunity to attend the University of Cambridge in the United Kingdom for his master's degree in mathematics. He later would enroll at Columbia University for his Ph.D. on full scholarship as well.

I credit Our Lady for holding his hand and guiding him as he pursued both music and mathematics at a high level. I eventually realized that God had a perfect plan in place all along for Anthony, even when he first embraced the cross of having to live with type 1 diabetes.

Just six years later, my daughter Gianna Marie was also diagnosed with type 1 diabetes. She and I pray a decade of the Rosary together in the car on the way to school, and I know God will always take care of her. It is amazing how God works. Anthony's struggles with diabetes helped his sister to accept her condition more easily. In turn, after a few years, Gianna volunteered as a counselor at a local diabetes summer camp. She became a youth lector and altar server, and as a freshman, she attended the March for Life in Washington, DC; became quarterback of the girls' varsity flag football team; and was named an Excelsior Scholar at one of the top ten Catholic high schools in the nation. Glory to God in the highest!

In addition, my daughter Courtney has told me countless times how she recognized God's hand in her life and attributes much of this to praying to the Blessed Mother. Courtney served in Catholic Campus Ministry (CCM) during college at the University of Central Florida. During a CCM retreat, she and a wonderful Catholic young man, Eduardo, became friends. They began their friendship committing to praying the Rosary together for thirty consecutive days during the month of Mary. They are now engaged to be married. I am so grateful to Mother Mary for helping lead my daughter to Eduardo, who is from a very devout Catholic family that also has special devotion to Our Lady.

Mary, Our Heavenly Mother, is always there for us, ready to hold our hand and guide us. She is waiting for us to call upon her and to ask for her intercession. God sends His Mother to our aid, and she then draws us closer to her Son. She is the perfect model of how to accept suffering and surrender to God's will in difficult times. I can see that now. Thank you to Our Lady!

REFLECTIONS

———

FROM SCRIPTURE

"We know that all things work for good for those who love God, who are called according to his purpose." (Romans 8:28)

———

QUESTIONS

How is your relationship with your Heavenly Mother Mary?

Do you ever ask for Mary's intercession in times of need?

How often do you pray the Rosary? Do you wish you could pray it more often? If so, how might you make the time?

When difficulties come, do you believe that "all things work for good for those who love God, who are called according to his purpose" (Rom. 8:28)?

Do you believe God listens to and answers your prayers?

Melting Hearts and Miraculous Healings

BY KRISTINE HASS

WORDS OF WISDOM

*Though your prayers may not always be
answered the way you want or at the time you
desire, never doubt the power of Jesus to heal.*

SAINTLY ADVICE

*"Worry is a weakness from which very few
of us are entirely free. We must be on guard
against this most insidious enemy of our peace
of soul. Instead, let us foster confidence in God,
and thank Him ahead of time for whatever He
chooses to send us." (Blessed Solanus Casey)*

KRISTINE STEWART HASS, a longtime professional communicator, is the director of faith and family formation for St. Joan of Arc Church and an advocate and interventionist for children with dyslexia. The parents of five children, she and her husband Richard reside in St. Clair Shores, Michigan. Her websites are www.readteam.org and FiveHalos.com.

W hat are you doing, silly girl? Flying?"
I asked that question one July morning in 2018 when, mid-sentence, our eleven-year-old daughter stopped talking and started flapping her arms. Within a few seconds, she stopped and was back to her chatty self. My husband Richard and I didn't think anything of it until a few days later, when she did it again.

"Mom, Lillian is being a faker," our eight-year-old son, Cliff, reported. "She's making her arms twitch."

Soon enough, these perplexing moments occurred daily. Shortly after Lillian woke up, they'd come in clusters of four or five within minutes of each other. It became apparent she had no idea they were happening. She'd zone out for anywhere from about seven to thirteen seconds, flap her arms at waist height, and then go back to her normal cheerful self, albeit somewhat tired out.

She became aware something was awry when she had one of these moments while holding a paper cup filled with water. She didn't drop the cup, but water went everywhere. After I informed her what we saw, she said, "I thought something was going on, because I've been noticing you all staring at me."

After a visit to the pediatrician, then a neurologist, and a series of tests, we learned our joyful, sunshiny, easygoing girl's life was about to change. Dramatically.

Lillian was diagnosed with myoclonic-absence epilepsy. It turned out she experienced as many as fifty absence seizures a day, during which she'd lose consciousness for a few seconds. In addition, she experienced morning clusters of myoclonic-absence seizures. That's why her arms would elevate and move rhythmically.

The absence seizures (which used to be called petit mal seizures) explained a lot, especially Lillian's frequent "daydreams," after which she'd ask questions we had just answered. Such seizures aren't terribly uncommon among children and often go away. But the myoclonic involvement and the age of onset made Lillian's condition much rarer.

"She may never drive," her doctor said. "She can only swim with a one-on-one designated lifeguard. She should always have someone with her when she crosses the street. She should have a buddy to walk with at school, especially up and down stairs. No climbing trees." The litany of restrictions went on.

Medication changed Lillian. She was constantly exhausted, living in fear of her next seizure, and the sparkle completely disappeared from her pretty blue eyes, leaving them flat and sunken deep within dark circles. She lost her confidence and happy-go-lucky disposition. Even with the cocktail of medications, Lillian had a cluster of seizures every five or six days. We put an emergency plan in place at home and at school for the tonic-clonic (grand mal) seizures we were told to expect.

"We might only be able to get this managed," her doctor said.

Desperate for help, my husband and I turned to St. Valentine for intercession. It turns out the patron saint of love is also the patron saint of epileptics. Who knew?

A few weeks before Valentine's Day, I privately asked friends and family if they would be willing to send our sweet Lillian a Valentine's Day card to let her know they were praying for her and asking for St. Valentine's intercession. To my great surprise, our mailbox overflowed. More than 250 people responded with cards, coloring pages, gifts, stories, and prayers. I reminisced with Lillian about each person who responded. As much as Lillian's heart was filled, my husband and I were flooded with joyful memories of childhood buddies, college friends, former co-workers, and people we knew from church. For weeks, our mailbox offered daily sentimental trips down memory lane.

A few weeks after Valentine's Day, we decided to make the hour-long trek to Brighton, Michigan, to take Lillian to a healing service at St. Patrick's Catholic Church hosted by the Encounter School of Ministry. As a family, we'd attended (and loved) Encounter conferences, where we'd witnessed miraculous healings and heard amazing testimonies. For whatever reason, though, Lillian rejected the idea of going to a healing service. That may sound typical for a kid, but it wasn't for Lillian. She was always so agreeable and loved to go anywhere as a family, but she put on the brakes at this suggestion and only begrudgingly agreed in the end. She put on a winter ski cap and oversized clothing, almost as if she were hiding. She insisted we sit at the very back of the church (which we never do).

During the service, the leaders prayed for corporate healing and called out various ailments afflicting certain parts of the body. Healing ministers shared their words of knowledge, none of which applied to Lillian's condition. She withdrew even more. When prayer teams took up their places around the church, we got in line, in spite of Lillian's insistence that she was fine and just wanted to go home.

When Lillian's turn came, she sat surrounded by five prayer ministers, my husband Richard, and our son Cliff (who loves to pray for healing). Because I was very cognizant of Lillian's reluctance, I chose to stand back and observe. I couldn't hear all that was said, but I watched the angst melt from my daughter. As she sat with her eyes closed, for the first time in months, I saw the radiance that had been missing from her sweet face.

After the ministers prayed, she thanked them with hugs. Unlike our drive to the service, our trip home was joyous. We chatted as we searched for an open restaurant. It was late and we were all so hungry. Our server at the empty Cracker Barrel commented on our late-night joy. We told her about the service, we prayed for her, and she wept, saying God knew just what she needed that night.

Once our food came, Lillian shared her experience. She said when the ministers were praying for her, she felt overwhelmed with peace.

"I saw Jesus in my head with scissors, cutting the strings of epilepsy," she told us.

This was remarkable, especially since, at that point, Lillian didn't really understand the neurological basis of her epilepsy. She felt such peace. Full of hope, we sang praise and worship songs the whole drive home.

Did she have more seizures? Yes. She wasn't miraculously healed—yet.

A few months went by; medications were adjusted; results were the same. Another Encounter healing service was scheduled at a nearby parish, and we decided to go again. Lillian agreed but refused to wait for a team to pray over her. She wept and cried out, "Why don't they call out the problems with my brain in the corporate prayer?"

I did my best to assure her that Jesus heard our prayers.

Two weeks later, while in my bedroom preparing to sing at the Easter Vigil, I heard the telltale sound of an earring hitting tile. Lillian was in the bathroom getting ready to serve at Mass with her brothers. From outside, I saw her have a cluster of three eight-to-ten-second seizures while looking in the mirror. That was unusual at that time of day, but she continued seizing, unaware. I retreated to my bedroom to continue dressing. Then, I heard the thud.

I opened the bathroom door to find my husband cradling Lillian on the ground as the seizure continued. The length of her seizure—over a minute now, the longest she'd ever had—and the movement of her arms had slowly caused her to fall and lightly hit her head against the doorframe, causing the thud I heard. Luckily, Richard was there to catch her.

When Lillian came to, she looked up at us and smiled, her eyes sparkling.

"Hi, Mommy! Hi, Daddy! Did I have a seizure?"

My husband and I looked at each other, and at that very moment, I became overwhelmed by the presence of angels. On the wall, right above our heads, was a plaque that read, "Holy Spirit, you are welcome here." The moment was surreal and the picture of it all is cemented in my memory.

Although we decided it would be best for Lillian to leave the altar-serving to her brothers, she insisted on attending the three-hour vigil Mass. I assumed she would fall asleep. As cantor for the Mass, I sang from the choir loft, then cried, then sang, and then cried some more, all while pleading to the Holy Spirit to help our beautiful girl. At the end of Mass, I was surprised to find Lillian chipper, chatty, and sunshiny. Her eyes sparkled, and she radiated joy.

First thing Easter Monday, I headed to the Solanus Casey Center in Detroit, wrote Lillian's name in the prayer book, and begged Blessed Solanus Casey for his intercession. Despite Lillian's long seizure only two days before, I was overcome with relief as I prayed.

And that was it. That was her last seizure. That was the last time she experienced side effects from her medication, even though her dose had not changed. Just like that, our Lillian was back. After six seizure-free months, she began tapering off her medication. A twenty-four-hour EEG confirmed she was in absolutely perfect shape. Our doctor was amazed and asked what we were doing. Lillian and I looked at each other and said, "Going to healing services and praying."

A year has passed since that last doctor's visit. Lillian took St. Valentine as her Confirmation saint. She shares her testimony and boldly acknowledges that she is the recipient of a miraculous healing. She also willingly attends healing services and offers prayers of healing for others. Most importantly, she knows with confidence that all the glory of her story goes to the amazing healing power of Jesus.

REFLECTIONS

———

FROM SCRIPTURE

"Everyone in the crowd sought to touch him because power came forth from him and healed them all." (Luke 6:19, NABRE)

———

QUESTIONS

Do you believe in miracles? Do you think they happen only to those who are very advanced in holiness and have a deep relationship with God?

How often do you study miracles associated with the saints?

What miracle or answer are you looking for right now?

Have you thought about "thanking God ahead of time," as Blessed Solanus Casey suggests?

I Want You to Walk with Me

BY ELLEN SALTER

WORDS OF WISDOM

A quiet and obedient heart gathers the grace and wisdom showered upon us by the Holy Trinity. Redemptive suffering brings you into the merciful heart of Jesus, where you will find authentic peace.

SAINTLY ADVICE

"Do not fear, My little child, you are not alone. Fight bravely, because My arm is supporting you; fight for the salvation of souls, exhorting them to trust in My mercy, as that is your task in this life and in the life to come." (Words of Jesus to St. Faustina Kowalska, Diary, no. 1452)

ELLEN SALTER is a pro-life speaker whose greatest passions in life are serving Jesus, caring for and loving her family, and defending every soul's right to life as a gift from God. Ellen's daughter, Meghan, has an undiagnosed medical condition that renders her unable to eat, speak, move, or breathe on her own. Meghan, who wasn't expected to live past six months, is now eighteen years old. She has been on life support since she was an infant and is cared for at home. Ellen boldly defends life, speaking out for the handicapped, weak, and vulnerable in our society, as well as opposing euthanasia. Through Scripture and prayer, she offers her family's sufferings to the heart of Christ. Learn more about Meghan at MeghansMiracles.com.

My husband, Mike, and I were blessed with a beautiful marriage. We had two healthy children, Lauren and Michael, and life was just grand! We were joyfully expecting our third child. Darkness overshadowed us when, at twenty-two weeks gestation, our baby nearly died. We were brought to our knees, begging for our baby to live. We would accept and love any baby, healthy or ill, that Jesus gave us.

Our prayers were answered. After thirteen weeks of lying on my left side, requiring Mike to care for us all, I delivered a beautiful, healthy baby girl, whom we named Shannon. We didn't realize then that Jesus was preparing our hearts for the plan He had in mind for us.

Often, I sat alone before the Blessed Sacrament in the small chapel of my childhood parish in Dearborn, Michigan. There, I would hear Our Lord and Our Lady quietly call out to me. In the same soft voice, they both always asked one question: "Will you accept a special-needs child?"

My answer was the same every time. Immediately, in a resounding voice, I said: "Yes, I would be the mother of any child you have for me. In fact, I want to be the mother of the child that *no one wants*, a child that might be killed in an abortion due to his special needs." Clearly, the Holy Spirit inspired me.

Neither did this call upset me nor did I dwell on it. Just the opposite: I felt truly honored that Our Lord and Our Lady would consider entrusting to Mike and me a child in need of special care. I did not know for certain whether Jesus would bless our family with a healthy or a special-needs baby. Jesus and Mary did not reveal any details to me, and in all fairness, I never asked any questions. For all I knew, they were just asking to see how pro-life I was. Did I truly have an obedient heart?

I couldn't help but reflect on the Annunciation. To my knowledge, the angel Gabriel did not show Mary her crucified Son, and she did not ask what would happen to her. She was called and freely said yes. Perhaps pondering the Annunciation caused my heart to respond this way to Jesus and Mary. I felt the Holy Spirit rush through me each time I heard their voices. I was unafraid, joyful, and humbled to the core just to hear them. Again, God was preparing my heart for what was to come. He chose, prepared, and called us to be pro-life in sickness and in health, to cherish every life as a unique soul created in His image!

Soon, Mike and I were expecting again. Our hearts were bursting with joy. We were blessed to be the parents of a beautiful daughter, Meghan. She was born healthy, but her strength soon started to decline. To this day, she is unable to speak, move, eat, or breathe on her own. She has been on life support since she was a few months old. She has taken many medical flights and has spent countless months in intensive care units. Although she has suffered many airway collapses that nearly took her life, we have witnessed her determination to live, and we have experienced God's mercy as He spared her life again and again.

Now eighteen, Meghan is currently not in pain and has a smile that touches every soul she encounters. Through the abundant grace of the Holy Trinity, she is the joy of our family, loved by people around the world. Jesus has an extraordinary plan for her to assist Him in bringing souls to His most merciful heart. Through intense prayer with a local Catholic priest and bishop, we learned from God that He chose Meghan to suffer for souls on a more intimate level than we could begin to imagine. Meghan is keenly aware of her work for Jesus and continues to say yes to her mission of uniting herself with Christ and saving souls for the eternal kingdom.

The way our family suffers while remaining joyful has been shaped by one amazing encounter I had with the Lord. Brace yourself as I tell you this story.

At the time, every indication was that Meghan was dying. We were tearfully begging for Jesus to spare her life and heal her. In return, we would renew our promise to care for our ill child, and I would travel the world telling every soul I met about my Lord and His eternal love.

Amid our suffering, we very intentionally coddled our children and kept their eyes fixed on Jesus. Mike was the best at making sure Lauren, Michael, and Shannon felt intense love every minute of the day. On a day Jesus chose, Mike took our three older children out for ice cream. I knew I would have only a small sliver of time alone with Meghan. Unaware of what was about to happen, I sobbed, and I began to pray out loud as I rocked her. I called out to Mother Mary, St. Joseph, Fr. Solanus Casey, Jesus, and God the Father.

"I need you right now to come to me," I said.

Immediately after I called their names, Our Lady, St. Joseph, Fr. Solanus, and my Lord stood in a line across from me, in the exact order I called them. I was so weak, desperate, and frail, but I kept praying.

"Blessed Mary, please hold me and please don't let me fall," I said. "If I fall, I'm afraid I will never get back up." I needed her strength in every area of my life.

Next, I called out, "St. Joseph, please guide and protect Mike, for he needs to be the pillar of our family." I knew Mike needed this great saint to give him all the gifts required to hold our family together during this agony.

Next in line was our dear Fr. Solanus, now Blessed Solanus Casey. I begged him for the miracle of extending Meghan's life and, should it be God's will, completely healing her.

Then, there was Jesus, completing the Holy Family. I had given the three previous saints a mission, a "job," if you will. However, when I called in desperation to my King, my heart changed, and my words became not a favor but a question. With a sincere heart full of love, devotion, and obedience, I asked, "Jesus, what do you want of *me?*"

Jesus, in all His glory, stepped out of line and walked over to me. With great love, He stretched out His warm, strong hand and took mine, lifting me up. He called me by name. He said to me, "Ellen, I want you to walk with me."

With this, my small living room changed into a scene new to my eyes: a seashore. The sand and water stretched as far as I could see. I was walking barefoot where the water and sand met, and Jesus was close beside me. The path before us was long and full of curves. We proceeded together, hand in hand. There I was with my Savior, my Shepherd. The Lord of Lords, King of Kings, and Prince of Peace was accompanying me, His daughter, His little lamb. I dare not explain in words the overwhelming joy and peace that fills me to this day.

Jesus created a very winding path for our journey together from that day forward. I asked Jesus to show me the end of the path. I desperately wanted to know if Meghan would live a while longer or be called home soon. Jesus, in all His mercy, answered me without words. He made it known that it was not His will to reveal the answer I so longed for. That day, He gave me Himself. He invited me to walk with Him and hold His hand. And believe me, He has never once let go! To this day, I can feel His warm, strong hand holding me, His beloved daughter.

How precious to me are your thoughts, O God!
How vast the sum of them!
If I would count them, they are more than the sand.
When I awake, I am still with you (Ps. 139:17–8).

REFLECTIONS

—

FROM SCRIPTURE

"And though the Lord give you the bread of adversity and the water of affliction, yet your Teacher will not hide himself any more, but your eyes shall see your Teacher. And your ears shall hear a word behind you, saying, 'This is the way, walk in it,' when you turn to the right or when you turn to the left." (Isaiah 30:20–21)

—

QUESTIONS

Have you ever said yes to Jesus without knowing the reason for His question or the cross He might ask you to bear?

Have you ever made a sacrifice that
brought you into a more intimate
relationship with God? How has this
changed your heart and view of suffering?

Have your past sufferings brought you
closer to God, or have you become hard-
hearted, lost faith, or fallen into despair?

Were you ever surprised by the joy
that took over your heart when you
totally surrendered to God?

Do you call on Jesus, Our Blessed
Mother, and the saints when you need
help in a difficult situation, or do you
rely on your own truths for insight?

23

Bridge to Heaven

BY MARCY KLATT

WORDS OF WISDOM

*Prayers, Masses, and devotions such the Rosary and the Divine Mercy
Chaplet are effective. God works in many ways, often very subtle ones.
If we are open to the Holy Spirit, we can see His work and His graces
in our lives and those of others. He uses the people and circumstances
around us to bring us closer to Him. He wants us to know His love and
mercy and to be near Him. The most important thing is to trust Him,
be at peace, and accept His will in our lives. Jesus, I trust in you.*

SAINTLY ADVICE

*"At the hour of their death, I defend as My own glory every soul that will
say this chaplet; or when others say it for a dying person, the indulgence
is the same. When this chaplet is said by the bedside of a dying person,
God's anger is placated, unfathomable mercy envelops the soul, and the
very depths of My tender mercy are moved for the sake of the sorrowful
Passion of My Son." (Words of Our Lord to St. Faustina, Diary, no. 811)*

MARCY KLATT has a bachelor's degree in telecommunications from the University of Florida's College of Journalism. She has worked for more than thirty years in media including television production, social media, promotions, digital marketing, and public relations. She is a webmaster and specializes in social media and digital communications. An avid reader, Marcy is known as the Catholic Book Lady on Facebook and Twitter. She volunteers her time as a lector, webmaster, and social media manager for her parish in South Florida, where she lives with her family. She is currently in formation to become a Secular Discalced Carmelite. She occasionally blogs at LiveCatholic.net.

My husband, John, started having trouble with his health right after the coronavirus shutdown started in March 2020. His doctors started doing tests and running extensive blood work. A few weeks later, the Saturday after Easter, his lung collapsed, and I rushed him to the emergency room. I also contacted everyone I thought would pray for him. My pastor immediately put him on the Mass list and began praying for him during the parish's livestreamed Masses. My Bible study went into action. Friends and prayer groups started praying for John and arranging for Masses everywhere from Michigan to El Salvador. The sincere response from so many people astonished me. The Holy Spirit just seemed to be working everywhere.

We eventually discovered that a mass was blocking John's lung and, several days later, that he had stage four lung cancer. This was a surprise, since a routine CT scan taken nine months before was clear. The lung cancer specialist was very hopeful about new treatments, and a procedure was scheduled to unblock the lung and take tissue samples. It didn't go as the doctor hoped, however.

John was raised Presbyterian but wasn't interested in religion. He was a wonderful man, kind and hardworking, but it was painful for me that he neither shared my Catholic Faith nor had any religious practice. He was very supportive of whatever I wanted to do, but he didn't share my love for God.

During the twenty-six years of our marriage, I prayed many a Rosary and Divine Mercy Chaplet for John. Every Mass that I attended, I offered for him. My hope was that someday, we would be able to pray and receive the Eucharist together. His diagnosis and very quick decline ended that hope. Now, I simply wanted him to receive, somehow, a gift of faith.

During a drive to the doctor's office, I told John about the many people praying for him. He deliberately had not told any of his friends or co-workers he was sick, but here I had people praying for him internationally. I explained that our priest was saying Masses for him and that one Mass itself was worth more than all the prayers in the world. He was shocked. It seemed to mean a lot to him.

A few days later, I updated him about all the people, Catholic and Protestant, praying for him, and the many, many Masses people had arranged to be said for him. There were so many I had to keep a list, which he then asked for so that he could keep it nearby and look at it. One night at dinner, during grace before meals, when we pray for those in need, we prayed for him, and he astonished me by asking that we pray for all the people who were praying for him! I knew that Jesus was touching his heart somehow.

Just three days after his official diagnosis, I noticed just how weak John had become. He had to receive nebulizer treatments to help him breathe, but he was too weak to hold the nebulizer to his mouth. We had a virtual appointment with the pulmonologist who was to unblock his lung, and he agreed John needed to go to the ER immediately. The first time I took him to the hospital, he was hearty, walking quickly and easily to the coronavirus testing tent before entering the ER by himself. This time, two weeks later, I had to drop him off with a nurse, since I wasn't allowed in the hospital. He couldn't walk and needed a wheelchair. He was too weak to explain fully what was wrong, so I had to send him with a note explaining why he was there, as if he were a kindergartener.

The next day, fluid around John's heart had to be removed to help him breathe. The very painful procedure didn't do much, and I received a phone call from the pulmonologist explaining that there was nothing more they could do, as he wouldn't survive the unblocking procedure. He had an extremely aggressive cancer. Four specialists were shocked at how quickly it was progressing. The next step was hospice.

I was finally allowed to be with him only because he was dying. By the time I got through hospital security, he was already somewhat out of it. There would be no more exchanges of love and affection. No more chances to talk about things that mattered.

The next couple of days flew by. Originally, we expected that John would be able to come home, which he desperately wanted. From personal experience, I knew watching someone die at home could be heart-wrenching for a family, but this time was important. I was grateful that our priest would be able to visit him and give his blessing, even though John could not receive any final sacraments, since he was not Catholic.

It turned out hospice at home was not possible. His breathing was just too unstable and labored and his pain control too complicated for him to go home. Our sons were able to visit their dad and say their goodbyes, even though he could not talk with them, as the painkillers had him too medicated even to open his eyes. John's mother and sisters and a couple of his good friends were able to talk to him over speakerphone. And, finally, a local priest, not allowed to visit the hospital, said a blessing over him through FaceTime.

I stayed with him the first night, sleeping on a recliner in his room, talking to him, playing his favorite music, and praying the Rosary and Divine Mercy Chaplet. I had seen so many ties to the Divine Mercy devotion the last couple of weeks, and so I really made it my priority. John passed away the next day, exactly one week after his diagnosis. I was at his side, telling him Jesus was waiting for him, and he should walk into His arms, tell Him he loves Him, and accept His mercy.

Over the next few days and weeks, we were blessed by so much love and generosity, and for months, many people continued to pray and offer Masses for John. I felt I had done everything I could help him get to heaven, but of course, I wouldn't know until I got there myself. I still wondered if I had done enough, and if he really had the faith necessary.

Then, about six weeks after his death, a friend of mine who is a Secular Discalced Carmelite called me. She wanted to tell me about a dream she had about John a couple of weeks after his death. She told me the dream and I asked her to write it down for me. She wrote:

In the dream I saw John arriving in a white car and wearing a white shirt. He arrived to Heaven. As he got out of the car, right there was Jesus, standing, waiting for him with a big and joyful smile. Jesus was wearing a white tunic. Jesus said hello and welcomed him. John, smiling, said, "Hi, who are you?" Jesus said with a big smile, "I am Jesus." And John, with a big smile, too, said, "Oh, you are Jesus, the God of Marcy." Jesus looked at him with great love and, laughing, extended His hand to him. John laughed too, and extending his hand to Jesus, he crossed like a line that needed to be crossed in order to get to Jesus' side. I saw he had to jump a little bit, and Jesus somehow pulled his hand to help him jump. Jesus surrounded John's shoulders with His arms and they left together, talking and laughing.

She then told me that on the day of John's funeral, she had gone to my Facebook page, which is where we livestreamed his funeral for family and friends to watch. She had never met him or seen his picture before, but when she saw the pictures that I had posted of him, she was shocked.

"That's the man that was in my dream!" she realized.

She hadn't been able to see his face very well, but everything else about him was the same.

What an emotional moment for me. She said that this wasn't an ordinary dream that disappears into the ether as you awake, but a clear, sharp memory. A different kind of dream. Of course, interpreting dreams is no easy thing, but I think it was meant to give me reassurance that yes, indeed, Jesus is taking care of John and showering him with His mercy in a place of great joy.

I wonder about the little line he had to cross, and whether that was the chasm we supposedly pass over to get to heaven, and if perhaps all the prayers, Rosaries, and Masses said for John paved the way to make it easier to cross to the other side. I would like to think so.

REFLECTIONS

_____

FROM SCRIPTURE

"May the God of hope fill you with all joy and peace as you trust in him, so that you may overflow with hope by the power of the Holy Spirit." (Romans 15:13, NIV)

_____

QUESTIONS

What devotions are you particularly drawn to and why? (Examples might include the Rosary, Stations of the Cross, the Sacred Heart of Jesus, the Immaculate Heart of Mary, or Divine Mercy.)

How often do you practice this devotion, even if only in the car?

Is there a saint you admire or feel drawn to? Which saints do you want to learn or read about? Popular saints and their writings include St. Thérèse of Lisieux, the "Little Flower," and her autobiography, *Story of a Soul*; St. Augustine, whose many great works of theology and philosophy include his autobiographical *Confessions*; Mother Teresa of Calcutta and her testimony, *A Simple Path*; and St. Faustina, who recorded her conversations with Jesus in her *Diary: Divine Mercy in My Soul*. Learning about the saints and reading their works are powerful means of opening your eyes to the ways of the spiritual life and the journey toward heaven.

When you experience challenges, do you turn to God, for example, by talking to Him in prayer or by reading the Bible? Do you ask the saints to intercede for you?

Do you trust that God is listening when you speak to Him?

Before going to bed, do you ever reflect on or pray about the day, giving thanks when you recognize God's work in your life?

When someone you know suffers
a difficult time or a tragedy, how
do you respond? For instance,
do you make a phone call, mail a
card, or pray for the person?

Have you ever thought about
having a Mass said for loved ones
who are sick or have passed away?
What about for their caregivers?

24

Holy Neon Signs

BY KATHLEEN BORDO CROMBIE

WORDS OF WISDOM

Jesus tells us, "If any man would come after me, let him deny
himself and take up his cross and follow me" (Matt. 16:24).
Jesus never said discipleship would be easy, and indeed, it is not!
Regardless, He expects that at His loving invitation, we embrace
the cross in front of us and follow in His footsteps. The cross I
was sent in my forty-seventh year of marriage was a heavy one.
It required sacrificial surrender and trust. As I look back, I
understand fully that God had prepared me for this heavy cross.
We serve such a loving and merciful God. Jesus, I trust in you!

SAINTLY ADVICE

"Let us remember that love lives through sacrifice
and is nourished by giving. Without sacrifice,
there is no love." (St. Maximilian Kolbe)

KATHLEEN BORDO CROMBIE was married to Robyn Crombie for forty-seven years until his death in March 2020. She is a mother of two grown sons and grandmother to four beautiful grandchildren. Kathleen writes and speaks about her Catholic Faith, religious iconography, and pro-life issues. After eighteen years as the director of multicultural outreach and gift planning for Right to Life Michigan, Kathleen retired to spend more time with her family, travel the world, deepen her Catholic Faith through study and pilgrimages, and continue commissions and special projects as a working iconographer.

Kathleen is a volunteer for the Servants of Jesus of the Divine Mercy and the Divine Mercy Center, as well as an active member of the board of directors for the Michigan Chapter of the Patrons of the Arts in the Vatican Museums. She serves as a lector and Eucharistic minister at her parish, the Church of the Divine Child in Dearborn, Michigan. Kathleen is also working toward consecration as a Marian Catechist (if it is God's will).

Kathleen is an accomplished iconographer. Her icons can be found in several private collections, chapels, and churches, including the Cathedral of the Most Blessed Sacrament in Detroit. She can be reached at dignityoflife@yahoo.com.

February 2020 was a time of prayer and preparation for a thirty-day at-home Ignatian retreat, which I began on March 1. The Spiritual Exercises of St. Ignatius of Loyola focus on discernment and call the retreatant to resolve earthly attachments. On the sixth day of the retreat, before the evening meditation, I was beginning to prepare dinner for my husband Robyn and myself, when he came home from the health club and told me that he was unable to catch his breath. He also felt a tightening across his chest and a pain in his jaw—two things he had never experienced. He chewed two aspirin just in case he was having a heart attack. He ruled out calling an ambulance, but did agree to let me drive him to the nearest emergency room, which was just three miles away.

The staff admitted him immediately upon our arrival. An EKG revealed that he was, indeed, having a heart attack. He was alert and talking, when all of a sudden, his eyes rolled back in his head and he slumped down on the examination table. He had stopped breathing. The medical team began chest compressions as I stood nearby, trying to figure out what just happened. After a while, Rob's heart restarted. This happened at least three times, as I recall, within forty-five minutes or so.

Meanwhile, I frantically made phone calls to my sons, Derek and Chad. Without delay, they came to meet us. I also put out texts and phone calls to my team of prayer warriors, telling them where we were and what happened to Rob. I told them that he needed lots of prayers, and fast, as his life was on the line.

One of those faith-filled friends was Cindy. She was attending a fundraiser for our parish high school. When our associate pastor, Fr. Matt, walked in and sat down next to her, she immediately told him that Robyn Crombie had just had a heart attack and that he was in the ER nearby. Fr. Matt called me and said he was on his way. Within minutes, he arrived and administered Anointing of the Sick and the Apostolic Blessing even as the medical team continued chest compressions. Then, Fr. Matt led us in praying the Chaplet of Divine Mercy. This was really happening. I felt completely helpless.

Finally, the doctors stabilized Rob for an ambulance ride to the hospital's main campus downtown, where a cardiologist was awaiting his arrival. Before we left, I said thank you to what seemed like twenty health-care professionals in the room. One of the doctors commented that Rob experienced everything that could happen during a heart attack. It was unusual to see.

At the hospital, the cardiologist discovered that Rob's heart attack was massive and damaging. A stent was inserted into his artery to keep the blood flowing, but the doctors were worried about possible neurological damage. I decided to spend the night with Rob in the ICU and convinced my sons to go home and get some rest so they could relieve me for a short time the next day. Too anxious to sleep in the room's lounge chair, I prayed at my husband's bedside as best I could.

The next day was Sunday. At Mass, we all prayed for God's mercy and healing. Derek and Chad insisted I go home to freshen up and rest. While trying to sleep, I understood clearly that I should continue my retreat in the hospital. It would be my prayer to say at Rob's bedside.

I called my spiritual director to discuss the situation and request his prayers. If I could find a quiet place for meditation, he said, I could continue the retreat. Once Rob woke up, we would decide how to move forward.

After hanging up, I bundled up my books, my Bible, and my tablet and wireless keyboard for journaling and headed back to the hospital, where I learned that Rob's prognosis had become more complicated. The cardiologist on staff explained that with this kind of heart attack and now a lung infection, Rob had about a 20 percent chance of recovery. That was certainly not what I was expecting.

The cardiologist's next question was about Rob's end-of-life wishes. Another "stop in your tracks" moment.

"We are Catholic, and we believe in the teachings of the Catholic Church," I said. "We always err on the side of life."

The cardiologist nodded his head. Before he left the room, I told him that I was praying for a miracle. I meant it. I had experienced miraculous healing once before, when Chad and I met Irving "Francis" Houle, who had the wounds of Christ in his hands. When Irving prayed over us, Chad was healed physically from Hodgkin's disease, and I was healed from spiritual indifference and disobedience, as I was then a disobedient and indifferent Catholic. Through this humble man from Michigan's Upper Peninsula (whose cause for canonization opened in June 2019), God showered healing and mercy upon us. I knew He could do so again.

The next day, Monday, was all about whether Rob would wake up. My sons and I fully expected him to do so. When tested several times, Rob blinked his eyes, and his pupils dilated, although much more slowly than the doctors would have liked. For the moment, they were satisfied.

As I sat beside Rob, I started the third retreat meditation of the day, titled the "Standard of Christ." The purpose of the meditation was to discern what it meant to be a true disciple of Christ. In an earlier meditation, I learned that the Cross is the banner, or standard, of Jesus Christ. I also learned that He fully expects us to surrender what we have for His glory and our holiness.

After many prayers, through tears, I journaled:

Since Christ has a mission for each of us, it is our job to find out what His will is for us. My vocation has been to be a wife and mother. But it looks like part of my vocation may change, unless you have a miracle in mind for Rob, Lord. I'm not ready for you to take him from me yet, but if that is your will then I surrender our guy back to you. Let me truly be your disciple through this really painful time in my life.... I pray I can always be a witness to you at every turn in my life, especially like these really hard ones ... and this one is definitely right up at the top of list. Give me strength, Jesus, to walk in your footsteps carrying my cross bearing your banner. You are a loving God, but you do require much from your true disciples. It's a choice to grow in holiness or stay the current course. Holiness is what I seek, not only for myself, but others as well (Fr. John Hardon says no one gets to Heaven on their own). And I realize that genuine discipleship has a personal cost associated with it. You ask for an internal detachment in our hearts of bearing all insults and wrongs; you ask to practice internal and external poverty; and through my witness, lead others to follow Jesus under this standard as well. This is a hard one to ask for, but may your will be done, Jesus.

Around one in the morning, two doctors shared with me the results of Rob's CT scan. The news was not good: he had global brain damage. I was crushed. My shock worsened when they explained that if he did wake up, which they did not expect, he would not be the man I knew.

Then, they asked about his preferences regarding continued care. I asked if he could breathe on his own. They said they didn't think so, but they could run a test to make that determination. I gave them permission to do so because my sons and I needed to know before we could make any further decisions.

About three hours later, I had another window to pray my retreat. This meditation described three classes of people: those who talk about following Jesus but do nothing, those who follow Him but make compromises, and those who achieve full surrender to follow Christ. Which one did I belong to?

I don't remember exactly what I read or prayed, but it was pretty clear to me that God was asking me to surrender my husband, the person to whom I was most attached, to Him. This was the moment of truth. Talk about squirming.

Deep down, I knew better than to tell God no. I've done that before, and it's always the wrong answer. This was a very hard meditation, as I wrote in my journal:

I see myself as the compromiser on some things, but I also see myself as the achiever in others. I'm probably more of the compromiser on most things, but an achiever on others with a desire to be the achiever in all things. As I continue to pray this retreat at Rob's bedside, and realizing that he may well die/God is calling him home, I am surrendering my will to God's and making His will mine. So if, Lord, your will is to take him home, I understand. If your will is to heal him, I understand that too, and it would be for your glory.

In the morning, Chad arrived early. I told him my retreat was over. It was obvious to me that God had prepared me for this particular time in my life. I invested the month of February in preparation for the retreat and spent only a part of March immersed in the retreat itself. My plan was to complete the entire retreat, not just the first ten days. But that morning, I understood that God's plan was not my plan, and suddenly, a great sense of peace came over me.

After consulting and praying with Fr. John, a holy priest and a dear family friend, we determined that no heroic measures needed to be taken if Rob could not breathe on his own. After running the test we requested, the doctors told us it was clear that Rob was not breathing. The moment of truth had arrived. We made the very hard decision to gather our family and remove Rob's breathing tube later in the afternoon.

By four o' clock, the entire family was together. Rob was ready for the journey. He was wearing my brown scapular on his wrist. The Servants of Jesus of the Divine Mercy had prayed the Chaplet of Divine Mercy at his bedside with a first-class relic of St. Faustina, and so many of our friends and family had offered prayers and Masses for him during his three days in the hospital. As we prayed, the Eucharist, in a pyx, was placed on Rob's chest twice. He received Anointing of the Sick and the Apostolic Blessing. This was the "happy death" we read about in the lives of the saints. We should all be so prepared to meet Jesus in the same way. What an incredible blessing! Thanks be to God!

All the while, a hospice doctor was standing by in case Rob began breathing on his own. We made it clear that everything would change if that happened, but in the end, it did not. Robyn Crombie passed into eternal life. It was finished.

Do I miss my husband? Absolutely. But I understand there is no such thing as chance or coincidence. Everything occurs according to God's providence—everything, even the timing of this story's composition. I began writing it on the vigil of Divine Mercy and completed it on Divine Mercy Sunday. I did not plan that! Without a doubt, our merciful God writes straight with crooked lines. God's mercy is inexhaustible and ever-flowing. Believe me when I tell you that God seeks us before we ever think to seek Him.

Looking back on Rob's hospitalization and death, I see God's hand in everything. If Rob's heart attack had occurred only a few days later, things would have been very different. We headed to the ER on March 6, and he died in a Detroit hospital on March 10—the first day COVID-19 cases were reported in Detroit and the state of

Michigan. Very quickly, the virus protocol caused enormous changes in hospitals throughout the metro area. We have all thought about how God allowed Rob to have the very best medical care available. God gave our priests and family the chance to pray over him and for him for three days and to be at his bedside when he died. Rob was not alone. And as the pandemic kicked into high gear, we also became very aware that God protected us from what was to become a highly contagious environment.

As we were discussing funeral arrangements with our parish priests, Chad told me: "Well, Mom, you did your job. You got Dad to heaven."

He took my breath away with that remark—I could hardly speak. My son was exactly right: the goal of marriage is to get your spouse to heaven. Thank you, Jesus!

During months of social distancing, one of the few things I was able to focus on was catching up on my Bible class homework. I immersed myself in reading the commentaries on Romans and Galatians, which were balm for my soul following Rob's death. Scripture brought me great peace and understanding just when I needed it.

Near the beginning of my Ignatian retreat, while meditating, I clearly saw an image of a pen in my fingers, ready to write. As someone who does not usually see images during prayer, I considered this a big deal. I wondered if God wanted me to write the book that has been on my to-do list for some time. Maybe He was nudging me to get back in the studio and begin writing icons again. After Rob died, it became clear. Although Teresa Tomeo did not know about the image I had, she invited me to write a chapter for this book. And if that wasn't enough, I also received a call about the possibility of my writing a commissioned icon of the Holy Family. Chance? I think not. I use the gifts God gave me to serve others, but they have been a source of mercy for me, too, during this period of seclusion: with all my work, I have had no time to wallow in extended grief or loneliness. God is so good. He knows exactly what we need and when.

Mercy has also come in the form of great peace. Although we all miss Robyn very much, we are aware that, having received Anointing of the Sick and the Apostolic Blessing, Rob is definitely in God's hands, if not already in the arms of the Father for all eternity. What a great comfort that is to all of us.

I continue to pray to know God's will for my life so that I may follow Him better. I also pray for Him to send me neon signs so I don't miss what He's trying to tell me. Jesus says: "Ask, and it will be given you; seek, and you will find; knock, and it will be opened to you. For every one who asks receives, and he who seeks finds, and to him who knocks it will be opened" (Matt. 7:7-8). Jesus does these things for us and more. Everything He says is true. Count on it!

My Lord and my God, thank you, thank you, thank you for your love and mercy and the holy neon signs you send. Amen.

REFLECTIONS

———

FROM SCRIPTURE

"My grace is sufficient for you, for my power is made perfect in weakness." (2 Corinthians 12:9)

———

QUESTIONS

When was the last time you made a retreat to be with the Lord? Is He calling you to spend some time with Him again?

Do you truly believe in God's providence, that is, that nothing happens by chance or coincidence? If not, why?

St. Ignatius talks about the three classes of people in his Spiritual Exercises. Are you someone who talks about following Christ, but does not follow through? Do you follow Christ, but with compromises? Or do you fully

and totally surrender everything you
are and possess to follow Christ?

Do you understand and embrace
the Church's teachings on
end-of-life decisions?

Are you aware of the great graces
and blessings offered for the sick
and dying in the Sacrament of
Anointing of the Sick? Do you know
about the Apostolic Blessing?

Guidelines for Hearing and Discerning the Voice of God

BY TERESA TOMEO

Now that you have taken the time to read and ponder the many ways God chooses to speak to us, here are some guidelines for hearing and discerning the voice of God in your own life. As you'll see, our contributors followed most if not all of these steps. By doing so, they became open to what God had to say and applied His words to the various circumstances and situations of their lives.

The great news is this isn't rocket science. You don't have to be a theologian in order to establish a strong relationship with

God. Like any important relationship, our relationship with God requires dedication and attentive listening, communicating, and responding. Too often, we treat God, the author of life, like a slot machine. We put in our tokens; we say a prayer; we go to church; we await immediate answers and rewards from the spiritual one-armed bandit. Hopefully, we can see how treating loved ones and close friends this way would quickly damage those connections. God, of course, will never abandon us. But as St. Teresa of Avila says: "Christ does not force our will. He only takes what we give Him, but He does not give Himself entirely until He sees we yield ourselves entirely to Him." And that is where it all begins, with submission and surrender.

Put God first. Commit or recommit your life to Christ. Every day, tell God: "Lord, here I am. I have come to do Your will." Do this even if you haven't quite figured out what God's will for you is just yet. That's okay. Just keep offering yourself to Him. This is the first and most important step to take. God must come first for everything else in your life to fall into place. "Our hearts are restless," St. Augustine said, "until they rest in thee."

I never wanted to be in Catholic media. I was not even aware that Catholic media existed at the time I heard God's call to leave secular media. I blocked the signals I was receiving. Doors kept closing in the secular world, but I kept knocking on them, trying to force my way back in. I thought I had it all figured out when I landed a radio news director position. I convinced myself that I could stay in the news media, the only profession I thought I could do, and still fulfill God's will. But I wasn't thinking about God's will, only mine. Eventually, I realized after almost three years in a tug-of-war with God that He had other plans. He wanted to use my communication skills and gifts for His glory, not mine. Go figure. I have never looked back, and after twenty years in the Catholic media and communications arena, I've never been happier.

Spend time with Jesus in Adoration. The Church teaches us the Eucharist is the source and summit of our Faith. As Catholics, we are blessed not only to receive the Body, Blood, Soul, and Divinity of Jesus at Mass but also blessed to spend time with Him in Eucharistic Adoration. The Blessed Sacrament is exposed in a vessel known as a monstrance, allowing us to sit in our parish or chapel and spent quiet time literally with the Creator of the universe. If your parish does not offer Adoration, check with your diocese to find out where it is available. Nothing like some good "Sonshine" to help you hear from God.

Read the Bible daily. This is one of the most basic yet most important ways to establish a relationship with God and to hear from Him. Hebrews 4:12 tells us that God's Word is "alive and active. Sharper than any double-edged sword, it penetrates even to dividing soul and spirit, joints and marrow; it judges the thoughts and attitudes of the heart" (NIV). We keep in touch with those we love. We text, e-mail, meet on Zoom, or FaceTime. In other words, we're eager to hear what our loved ones have to say. If you want to hear from God, see what He has to say in Scripture. The daily readings for Mass are a great way to begin and to be in touch with the universal Church. Once you start reading Scripture, you might want to go deeper and get involved in a Bible study. Why not? You can never learn enough about our glorious God. The sky, or rather the universe, is your limit.

Silence the noise. If you wanted to have an important conversation with your child, spouse, or best friend, you wouldn't choose the loud pub down the street or a concert at the local arena. You would choose a quiet, most likely out-of-the-way place that allows at least some serenity and privacy. God deserves that much, and so do you. Find a quiet place to pray, read Scripture, or journal. Perhaps even carve out a little corner of your home or yard as your special place of prayer and retreat. Disconnect from technology and reconnect with God, even if you have only a few minutes.

Get to know the Holy Spirit. In His final exhortation to the apostles, Jesus promised us that although He was ascending to the Father, He would not abandon us.

If you love me, keep my commands. And I will ask the Father, and he will give you another advocate to help you and be with you forever—the Spirit of truth. The world cannot accept him, because it neither sees him nor knows him. But you know him, for he lives with you and will be in you. I will not leave you as orphans; I will come to you. (John 14:15–31, NIV)

The *Catechism* teaches us that we can be in touch with Christ only through the third person of the Holy Trinity, the Holy Spirit:

"God has sent the Spirit of his Son into our hearts, crying 'Abba! Father!' " This knowledge of faith is possible only in the Holy Spirit: to be in touch with Christ, we must first have been touched by the Holy Spirit. He comes to meet us and kindles faith in us. By virtue of our Baptism, the first sacrament of the faith, the Holy Spirit in the Church communicates to us, intimately and personally, the life that originates in the Father and is offered to us in the Son. (CCC 683)

Those are powerful and beautiful words. And all we have to do is say simply, "Come, Holy Spirit." While there are many incredible prayers to the Holy Spirit, all God wants is your yes. When you are about to pray, say, "Come, Holy Spirit." When you are getting ready to attend Mass, ask the Holy Spirit to open your heart to the readings and the message of the homily. As you open the Bible to see what God has to say to you in His Word on any given day, again say, "Come, Holy Spirit." And remember, God keeps His promises. The Holy Spirit is our advocate and will help you discern and hear God's voice more regularly and clearly.

Get to know the saints. The Catholic Church has canonized over ten thousand saints. These are men and women from all walks of life. None of them was perfect; each began as an ordinary person who did extraordinary things for the Faith. The saints teach us wonderful things about prayer, the Church, suffering, family life, overcoming sin, and more. They're great friends in heaven who want to help us get closer to God.

Continue to educate yourself about the Catholic Faith. As I have learned over the years, one could study the Church for an entire lifetime, and it would be merely, as the old saying goes, scratching the surface. Studying the Faith does not necessarily mean going to the local Catholic college or seminary. It could, if that's what you believe you're being called to do. But one of the great things about the media is the never-ending amount of resources available online. By visiting Catholic websites, even semi-regularly, you will get to understand more deeply Church teaching and how to apply it to your life and relationship with Christ. You can go online, for example, to the Vatican News site each week to see what the pope has to say. The possibilities for learning are endless.

Be truly open to what God has to say. God is never going to steer you in the wrong direction. He's God. He created us, loves us, and wants what's best for us, which is His will. It took me a long time to understand and accept that. I had to realize that like any good parent, God sometimes has to tell us no, even if we don't want to hear it. God will also never tell us that sin is okay.

Several years ago, one of my radio listeners sent me an e-mail asking for my opinion on her situation. She tried justifying her actions, which, very unfortunately, involved grave sin. She did not really want my opinion; she wanted confirmation from a Catholic talk-show host that everything was fine. She never answered my reply, in which I nicely but firmly told her that God would never affirm or encourage anyone to break one of His commandments. I tried not to be too heavy-handed, as I was really hoping to establish a dialogue. At the same time, all of us who know the truth of our Faith have a responsibility to explain and defend it and to help people avoid making harmful decisions.

On the positive side, the Holy Spirit was convicting her. That is why she contacted me in the first place. Something (or someone, namely, God) was forcing her to question her choices. Deep down, she knew she was wrong; otherwise, she would never have reached out. Had she kept in touch, I would have encouraged her first to go to Confession and then to seek spiritual direction to help her hear more clearly from God and avoid any near occasions of sin.

We see so much of this in our world today—folks want to tell God how things should be, instead of the other way around. We do not want to look into our hearts and see what needs addressing and mending. In my experience, it seems easier, at least at first, to keep going through life with little or no self-examination. But that causes us to put ourselves and God in a box. The prophet Jeremiah tells us that we will find God when we seek Him with all our heart (29:13). Again, a big part of hearing from God is being open to what He is trying to tell us. The more we seek Him, the more we learn not only about God but also about ourselves.

Have an attitude of gratitude. Regardless of your progress in hearing God, rejoice and be thankful that you want to be in relationship with Him and hear from Him more often. In our world today, there is so much busyness, clutter, and noise that continues to pull us away from God. Give thanks that you recognize your need and your longing to hear from Him.

Thank God for the little things and big things. Remember my story of thanking God for my statue of Jesus, the one with the words "Panis Angelicus"? I was pondering the amazing fact that decades after my First Holy Communion, I still had the little statue that meant so much to me. God then acknowledged my gratitude through the

"Panis Angelicus" hymn, which the cantor was singing at the very moment I thanked God for my statue. When I heard the hymn, I thanked Him all the more. See how it works? Keep thanking Him and watch how He says "Prego"—you're welcome—and showers you with His love, comfort, and guidance.

RECOMMENDED CATHOLIC RESOURCES

- Ave Maria Radio: https://avemariaradio.net/
- *Catholic Connection*: https://avemariaradio.net/program/catholic-connection/
- Catholic News Agency: https://www.catholicnewsagency.com/
- Catholic Scripture Study: https://www.cssprogram.net/
- Catholic Spiritual Direction: https://spiritualdirection.com/
- *Conquering Coronavirus*: https://teresatomeo.com/coronavirus/
- EWTN (Eternal Word Television Network): https://www.ewtn.com/
- *Magnificat*: https://us.magnificat.net/
- Marian Helpers: https://www.marian.org/amh/whoweare.php
- *National Catholic Register*: https://www.ncregister.com/
- Priests for Life: https://www.priestsforlife.org/
- T's Italy: (Catholic) Travel Italy Expert: https://www.travelitalyexpert.com/
- Teresa Tomeo Communications: https://teresatomeo.com/about/

- The Alexander House (Marriage Ministry): https://www.thealexanderhouse.org/
- *The Catholic View for Women*: https://www.thecatholicviewforwomen.com/
- *The Word Among Us*: https://wau.org/
- Vatican website: http://www.vatican.va/content/vatican/en.html
- WINE: Women in the New Evangelization: https://catholicvineyard.com/

Sophia Institute

Sophia Institute is a nonprofit institution that seeks to nurture the spiritual, moral, and cultural life of souls and to spread the Gospel of Christ in conformity with the authentic teachings of the Roman Catholic Church.

Sophia Institute Press fulfills this mission by offering translations, reprints, and new publications that afford readers a rich source of the enduring wisdom of mankind.

Sophia Institute also operates the popular online resource CatholicExchange.com. *Catholic Exchange* provides world news from a Catholic perspective as well as daily devotionals and articles that will help readers to grow in holiness and live a life consistent with the teachings of the Church.

In 2013, Sophia Institute launched Sophia Institute for Teachers to renew and rebuild Catholic culture through service to Catholic education. With the goal of nurturing the spiritual, moral, and cultural life of souls, and an abiding respect for the role and work of teachers, we strive to provide materials and programs that are at once enlightening to the mind and ennobling to the heart; faithful and complete, as well as useful and practical.

Sophia Institute gratefully recognizes the Solidarity Association for preserving and encouraging the growth of our apostolate over the course of many years. Without their generous and timely support, this book would not be in your hands.

www.SophiaInstitute.com
www.CatholicExchange.com
www.SophiaInstituteforTeachers.org